Introduction to Wills and Probate

As per Law in India

By Siva Prasad Bose

Published by Joy Bose

Contents

Dedication

This book is dedicated to all those people in India who have written a will or are thinking of writing a will.

Preface

Since the publication of the first edition of this work, fundamental changes have been incorporated into this second edition. These changes aim to ensure a clearer understanding of the subject, as this book serves as an introductory guide for dealing with wills and probate in India. It is intended to assist those who may not have prior knowledge of the laws governing wills and probate.

Everyone should have an up-to-date will that reflects an estate plan tailored to individual needs and circumstances. An estate plan is a thoughtfully designed arrangement for distributing one's assets to align closely with one's personal goals. Such objectives may include minimizing taxes, providing financial management for the surviving spouse and children, and selecting a trusted relative, friend, or advisor as executor or guardian. An estate plan can often be simple and inexpensive to prepare.

A will is typically a written document that takes effect upon the death of the testator—the legal term for the person creating the will. Its purpose is to distribute the testator's assets to the beneficiaries as per their wishes.

This text responds to a perceived need for a concise and comprehensive guide focusing on wills and probate, essential for the education of students and individuals dealing with the topics mentioned.

An objective of this book is to present the law and the court system as they function in practice. All relevant cases have been carefully selected and summarized to maintain their essence, providing readers with an accurate sense of judicial reasoning and decisions.

Note:

At various points, this book refers to Indian court judgments. For example, "AIR 1962 SC 567" refers to a Supreme Court judgment No. 567 from the year 1962.

Unless otherwise mentioned, "S-227" and similar references denote sections from the Indian Succession Act, 1925. Latin terms are italicized wherever they occur.

Case citations follow the standard Indian legal format. "AIR" stands for *All India Reporter*; "SC" denotes the Supreme Court of India; "Cal", "Bom", "Mad", "All", and similar abbreviations denote the relevant High Courts (Calcutta, Bombay, Madras, Allahabad, etc.). "SCC" refers to the Supreme Court Cases reporter, and "ILR" to the Indian Law Reports. References such as "S-63" or "Section 63" denote sections of the Indian Succession Act, 1925, unless another act is specified.

Acknowledgements

The author would like to acknowledge gratefully the following law books and references that were consulted:

- P.L. Parukh - Indian Succession Act, 1925 (11th Edition) by Justice K. Kannan.

- Indian Succession Act (4th Edition) by Sanjiba Rao.

- Hindu Law by Sir Dinshaw Fardunji Mulla (21st Edition).

- Fundamentals of Business Law – The Dryden Press by Rate Howell, John R. Allison, and N.T. Henley.

- Mogha's Indian Conveyancer (12th Edition).

- The Daily Telegraph: Everyday Law by Aviva Golden.

- Webster's Comprehensive Dictionary.

- Mulla T.P. The Indian Evidence Act, 1872, the Court Fees Act, 1870.

- Law of Wills by Indian Social Institute (Legal Education Personal Laws – 9): This booklet summarizes the salient features of the law of wills as contained in the Indian Succession Act in a question-answer format. It is advisable to keep this booklet handy when dealing with provisions related to wills/probate.

Chapter 1: Practical Considerations for Will Writing

In this chapter, we consider some practical considerations for a person considering making a will or estate plan.

1.1 What is a will and why should one make it

A will is a legal document declaring the intentions of a person regarding the distribution of their property after their death.

A will is one component of an overall estate plan, which documents how assets should be managed to realize one's wishes. These wishes include minimizing taxes, providing for surviving family members, selecting a trusted executor, and more.

If someone does not make a will and dies (intestate), their property will be distributed according to intestacy laws. These laws determine the distribution of property among the deceased's blood relatives. However, if the deceased intended to leave assets to charities, distant relatives, or friends, they would receive nothing unless specified in a will.

Reasons to make a will include:

- Revoking any previous wills.
- Identifying specific assets owned by the testator.
- Appointing guardians or setting up trusts for minor children.
- Nominating executors and trustees to manage assets.
- Preventing family disputes over property distribution.
- Leaving instructions for funeral arrangements, organ donation, or body disposal.

1.2 Intestate succession and testamentary succession

The Indian Succession Act 1925 is an act to consolidate the law applicable to intestate (dying without a will) and testamentary succession (succession where a will is present). The purpose of such a consolidating statute is to present the whole body of statutory law on a subject in a complete form, repealing the former statute.

The ordinary meaning of the word "succession" is a transmission by law or by the will of the man to one or more persons of the property and transmission rights and obligations of a deceased person. The federal court gave its opinion on a reference in the matter of the powers of the federal legislature to provide for the levy of an estate duty in respect of property other than agricultural land, passing upon the death of any person [AIR 1944 FC 73].

The law of succession is the law governing the transmission of property vested in a person at his death to some other person or persons.

In modern English law, the transmission occurs in two stages, namely:

- a passing by the operation of law to one or more representatives of the deceased person for the purpose of administration and

- a transference by the act of the representatives to the person entitled to the beneficial enjoyment [Parry's law of succession, Sixth Ed, p1].

1.3 What law governs

Succession in case of movable property:

In case of intestacy (dying without a will), the law of domicile at death determines who is entitled to succeed to the movables of the deceased. In the absence of proof of domicile elsewhere if a person dies in India, succession to his movable property is governed by the law of India.

In case of will of movables, the validity thereof will depend in general upon the law of the domicile of the deceased at the date of his death.

Succession in case of immovable property:

In order to be a valid disposition of immovable property, a will must be made in conformity with the law of the country in which the property is situated.

Therefore, when considering the question of validity of a will with regard to

- testamentary capacity of the testator,
- the heritable quality of the property, and
- the formalities and the constitution of a deed of will,

it is necessary to consider it with reference to the law applicable as laid down above. The country of domicile is the country of domicile at the time of making the will and subsequent change of domicile does not affect the validity of a previously made will.

1.4 Onus of proof in case of wills

As regards the onus of proof in case of wills, the rules of law are quite clear.

- The first rule is that the *onus probandi* lies in every case upon the party propounding a will, and he must satisfy the conscience of the court that the instrument so propounded is the last will of a free and capable testator.

- The second rule is that if a party writes or prepares a will under which he takes a benefit, or if any other circumstances exist which excite the suspicion of the court, and whatever their nature be, it is for those who propound the will to remove such suspicion, and to prove affirmatively that the testator knew and approved the contents of the will, and it is only where this is done that the onus is thrown on those who oppose the will to prove fraud or undue influence or whatever they rely on to displace the case for proving the will [1898, 25 Cal 824].

Reference may be made to the decisions [AIR 1977 SC 1202, 1962 3 SCR 195: Rani Purnima Vs Kumar Khagendra].

1.5 What is intestacy

a) A man is considered to die intestate with respect of all property of which

- he has not made a testamentary disposition e.g. when he has left no will

- he has made a will, but the will is not capable of taking effect e.g. when he has bequeathed his whole property for an illegal purpose, or if the subject of his bequest is non-existent.

Succession includes both intestate and testamentary succession [Bengal Act VIII of 1885]. The process by which one person succeeds another in the occupation or possession of any estate or the like [Section 25 or Section 26 of the Hindu succession act]: an order of descendants. In the law of descent, the coming in or another to take the property of one who dies without disposing it by will.

b) The word 'intestate' is defined in Section 55 of the administration of estates act [15 Geo SC 23] as follows: intestate includes a person who leaves a will but dies intestate as to some beneficial interest in his real or personal estate. Statutory nomination under special enactments like the PF Act, Payment of Gratuity Act 1972, the Insurance Act 1938, or a bank account [AIR 1928 PC 172]. It was held that nomination under the Government Savings Certificate Act 1959 did not operate as a third kind of succession which could be styled as a statutory enactment. A nominee could not be treated as being equivalent to a heir or legatee and therefore, the consent could be claimed by the heirs in accordance with the law of succession.

c) The person who dies 'intestate' – without having made out a will- already has a kind of will: state laws governing intestacy. These laws comprise a "standard" will reflecting the legislature's conception of the deceased's probable objectives. Under intestacy laws, property left by a deceased passes to survivors according to rules fixed by the deceased's state of residence.

d) Such rules never operate as an individual will made out according to a person's wishes. The rules frequently lead to serious shrinkage of the estate – and often to a distribution of assets quite different from what the deceased probably wanted. If the estate is large, long and costly litigation may follow the person's death. If the estate is small, it may be divided amongst various survivors in portions too small to help anyone. If the deceased leaves minor children, they will inherit part of the estate along with the widow.

e) The laws of intestacy provide in other ways for minor children. A guardian is usually appointed for the children, a process that involves expensive and time-consuming court proceedings. The guardian has to post a bond remunerable, annually, at a substantial premium. The guardian is supervised by the court and must account to it annually, resulting in more expenses and loss of time. All of these procedures are designed to protect the children and none take into consideration the fact that guardian may be the children's mother and the deceased's widow.

f) In brief, the time and expense involved in making out a will is infinitesimal in comparison with the problems that may come with intestacy. The "will you already have" is always inferior to the will you ought to have – even though the laws represent the state's best efforts to protect and provide for the survivors.

1.6 Cost of Writing and Executing a Will in India

The cost of drafting and executing a will can vary depending on complexity. Basic wills may cost between ₹2,000 to ₹10,000 if done through a lawyer. Registration fees at the Sub-Registrar's office vary by state. Professional executor services or consultation with estate planners may increase costs.

1.7 Role of Financial Advisors in Estate Planning

Apart from lawyers, financial advisors can help structure your estate to reduce taxes, plan asset allocation among heirs, and integrate financial instruments (e.g., life insurance, investments) with your estate plan.

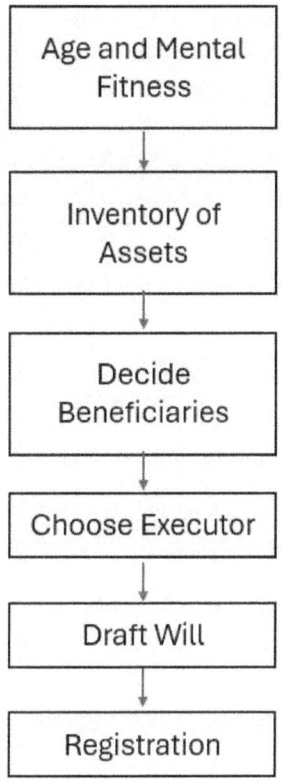

Figure: Checklist of key steps for writing a will

1.8 Conclusion

Understanding these practical considerations underscores the critical need for drafting a proper will. However, knowing these initial steps alone is insufficient. In the next chapter, we shall explore in detail the essential preparations needed before one's demise and the steps required to ensure the smooth handling of an estate after death.

Chapter 2: Death – Before and After

In this chapter, we discuss some steps a person should take to prepare for their death, in terms of their estate and funeral arrangements. We also consider the components of a will and the structure of a sample will.

2.1 Financial and legal aspects to consider before one's death

Following are some important financial and legal aspects related to the death of a person:

1. When someone dies, the partner or close relatives have to deal with a multitude of practical matters as well as coping with their emotions. In the short term:

- the death must be registered,

- arrangements should be made for the funeral,

- and the immediate day to day expenses of the dependents must be provided for, after which the affairs of the deceased person must be settled.

This means someone must take charge of his/her property, personal possessions, debts, business and so forth, which the law calls by the term "the deceased's estate".

2. No charge is to be levied for a medical certificate if the death was due to natural causes. One must register the death within five days with the concerned Registrar of births, marriages and deaths. The death is recorded in a register of deaths and a certified copy of the entry is called "the death certificate". Several copies of the death certificate need to be prepared for use in different places.

3. Arranging for the funeral: Funeral directors should provide one with the price lists and written estimates. Whoever arranges the funeral is responsible for payment. If the deceased left enough assets or cash, one

may be able to claim reimbursement out of the estate for reasonable funeral expenses.

4. Joint bank account: Personal accounts are frozen on death. Joint accounts can be operated provided that both the account holders are not required to sign every cheque. One can operate a joint account provided it needs a single signature.

5. The deceased's affairs:

(a) The deceased's papers: in order to find out if there is a will, one needs to go through the personal papers left by the deceased, check with his or her bank along with the past and present solicitors whether they hold his will. It might also have been deposited in the safe custody of the registry.

(b) Bank direct debits and standing orders / credit cards: One should check all direct debit mandates and standing orders. These cease on death if paid through a bank account in the deceased's sole name. One should make sure that all credit cards are returned with notice of death to the card companies, in order to avoid fraudulent misuse.

(c) The personal representatives who are the official representatives of the deceased to take charge of an estate:

To take charge of the deceased's property

To pay outstanding debts and taxes

To ascertain which persons are entitled to what is left

To ensure that beneficiaries are given their proper share

(d) A word of caution: if one deals with any property of a deceased person without any authority to do so, one can be liable to penalties.

2.2 Before death: Preparing for the inevitable

The choice is between leaving a will or dying intestate. A valid will ensures that a testator can determine what happens to our property after his death. If one does not make a will, i.e. one dies intestate, the law determines how his property will be distributed to whom and in what proportions.

2.3 Before death: Whether to make a will

Without a will, assets and belongings will be distributed on death according to the law of intestacy. The intestacy laws benefit blood relatives in the order of proximity, but charities and close friends get nothing. Good reasons, therefore, exist to make a will.

2.4 Before death: How to go about making a will

Any solicitor can prepare a will for you. The fees can vary from as little as Rs 50000 to 200000 depending on the following factors:

- Size of the estate

- The complexity of the will itself

It is advisable to confirm in advance with the solicitor how much would be the legal cost.

Note: If one nominates as executor a bank or similar organization or a solicitor or accountant, the will usually includes a clause that they will charge for their professional fees.

Alternatively, a person may choose not to use a solicitor and draft their own will.

Similarly, a person may choose whether to register his will at the sub-registrar's office or not.

The things to keep in mind after drafting one's will are as follows:

- Once a will is executed (written, signed and attested by two witnesses) it takes a legal form.

- It can then be kept in a safe place by the testator, to be opened after his or her death.

- It can also be kept at the sub-registrar's office (what is called a "registered will") for safety and record keeping.

- Note: Since the will may not be seen till after the funeral is over, it is a good idea to tell one's family and proposed executors about one's wishes in terms of the manner of one's funeral and organ donation, since this cannot be delayed

- A person may, before one's death, tell one's family members that he or she has signed a will and deposited for safekeeping in a probate court or bank

In the following sections, we consider the steps that should be taken by one's legal heirs after one's death.

2.5 After death: Finding the deceased's will

The following are the things to keep in mind for the legal heirs of the deceased, after the person's death:

•In some cases a person may die suddenly and the family members may be uncertain about the existence of a will and ignorance to its location if it exists. In such a case, they may conclude the person left no will at all, but this may not be correct.

•So in case of a person of education and reasonable net worth, it is good to begin a search for a will as soon as possible.

•One common place to keep a will is the safe deposit box of a bank that is rented by the person who writes the will.

•If the will is not located in the safe deposit box, the next step may be to enquire from the person's bank if they have nominated any person as executor.

•If this too does not bring results, one may search the person's home, including his personal papers.

•Once a will has been found after a person's death, it should be opened and read. Then it should be acted upon, with the most immediate and urgent items acted first.

2.6 After death: Obtaining authority to act - Probate

If the deceased leaves a will which names executors, the executors must apply to the probate division of the high court for grant of probate. If a will is made in duplicate, both parts must be lodged on a petition for probate. If there is no will, the administrators of the estate will be granted letters of administration by the same probate division to next of kin. Out of pocket expenses are always paid out of the estate. Approximately Rs 50000 to Rs 200000 may be required for payment to the advocacy/ court procedure.

2.7 After death: Dealing with the deceased's property

The function of the personal representatives is to take control of the deceased's property and land, as well as cash and personal effects. They will have to give a rough valuation of the house or flat which the deceased owned, to the probate registry. The figures will subsequently be checked by a valuation officer of the inland revenue. The amount or value of the property used in court fees refers to the net value of the property.

2.8 After death: Taking legal advice

One can instruct a solicitor, accountant or bank to deal with winding up the estate. Their fees can be substantial, so it is good to ask first about how much it might cost. If the deceased's affairs are straightforward, an ordinary person can deal with them. Executors can claim reimbursement of legal fees from the estate.

Executors are urged to open a separate bank account, known as the "executor's account", in order to keep a careful record of all payments in and out of the estate and to obviate any confusion with the executor's personal affairs.

2.9 After death: The deceased's creditors

The personal representatives are responsible for paying taxes and satisfying debts due by the deceased, out of the assets in the estate. Assets may have to be sold to raise cash in order to settle the debts, but beneficiaries under the will may have an interest in keeping particular assets of sentimental or other value.

2.10 After death: Paying the beneficiaries

If there are assets left over after paying the expenses, taxes and debts, the personal representatives must distribute them in accordance with the will.

2.11 Checklist of Documents Required After Death

- Death certificate
- PAN and Aadhaar card of the deceased
- Copies of the will (if available)
- Property documents
- Bank passbooks and account details
- Insurance policies
- Digital account credentials (if applicable)

2.12 Handling Digital Accounts and Online Services After Death

Family members should notify service providers (banks, email providers, social media platforms) and secure digital assets. It helps prevent identity theft and ensures closure of sensitive accounts.

2.13 Conclusion

Having considered the significant practical steps to take both before and after a person's death, it is essential now to gain a deeper legal understanding of wills themselves. The following chapter provides a detailed introduction to wills, their purpose, and their legal framework within the Indian Succession Act, 1925.

Chapter 3: Introduction to Wills

In this chapter, we discuss what is a will and what are its essential components.

3.1 What is a will

Will means the legal declaration of the intention of the testator with respect to the property which he desires to be carried into effect after his death [AIR 1967 Gujarat 214 / AIR 1966 MP 251].

A will is an instrument by which a person makes a disposition of his property to take effect after his death and which is in its own nature ambulatory and revocable during his life.

The Indian Succession Act 1925: it was an act to consolidate the law applicable to intestate and testamentary succession. The law of wills is contained in this act. It does not apply to Muslims and wills executed by Muslims are governed by the rules of Muslim Law.

Hindu law did not initially recognize wills. Sanskrit has no word for "Will". But the advent of the British India seems to have prompted Hindus, particularly in Bombay and Calcutta and in the Bengal presidency, to make wills. The practice spread to other places in course of time. Judicial decisions took note of this and gave it legal recognition. Ultimately the practice was given a statutory footing by legislation.

As mentioned, the will only takes effect on the testator's death and during his lifetime is an ambulatory document, revocable at any moment and having no legal effects whatsoever [Black's law dictionary].

As the most important tool used in estate planning, wills need always to be individualized to the creator's (or testator's) situation, estate and desires. The written will is signed by the testator in the presence of witnesses. It operates at his or her death to distribute property according to specifications in the document itself. The law imposes certain obligations, including the primary duty to pay tax liabilities, debts, funeral expenses and the cost of administration. The law also provides for a surviving spouse's legal rights in a decedent's estate and refuses to recognize, on public policy grounds, provisions discouraging marriage, wasting assets or tying up wealth for an unreasonable period of time.

3.2 Meaning of a will

Will is a translation of the Latin word "*voluntas*" which was a term used in the text of Roman law to express the intention of the testator. It is of significance that the abstract term has come to mean that document in which the intention is contained. It means the legal declaration of a man's intentions, which will be performed after his death. A last Will and Testament is defined to be "the just sentence of our Will, touching what we would have done after our death". Every testament is consummated by death, and until he dies, the will of a testator is ambulatory. A will is the aggregate of a man's testamentary intentions, so far as they are manifested in writing duly executed according to the statue. Under the General Clauses Act, a 'Will' includes a codicil and every writing making a voluntary posthumous disposition of property.

Will is a disposition of property made by a person during his life but intended to take effect after his death. It is defined in section 2(h) of ISA 1925, meaning "the legal declaration of the intention of a testator with respect to his property which he desires to be carried into effect after his death" [AIR 1967 Gujrat 214/ AIR 1966 MP 251].

Will is a secret and confidential document which the executant is never ordered to be produced [A 1949 PC 151]. A will takes effect on the death of the executant and during his lifetime is an ambulatory (means revocable subject to change: capable of alteration) document revocable at any moment, having no legal effect whatsoever [Black's Law Dictionary 1990 Edition p.80].

3.3 Purpose of the will

A will may be made for any of the following purposes:

- for disposal of the property of the testator after his death and for appointing an executor

- for appointing a testamentary guardian

- for exercising a power of appointment and

- for revoking or altering a previous will.

3.4 Essential characteristics of a will

Following are the three essential characteristics of any will

- There must be a legal declaration of the testator's intention

- The declaration must be with respect to the property of the testator

- The declaration must be to the effect that it is to operate after the death of the testator i.e. it should be revocable during the life of the testator.

If any of the above three essentials is lagging, the document is not a Will.

The will is a mere declaration of an intention so long as the testator is alive, a declaration that may be revoked or varied according to the variation in the intention, a disposition that requires the testator's death for its consummation and is but ambulatory or without fixed effect until the happening of that event.

3.5 Which law governs the will

The laws of the testator's state of legal residence determine the validity (or non-validity) of a will where personal property is involved. But because each state reserves the right to fix title to land situated within its boundaries, the law of the state where real property is located governs the validity and effect of the will with respect to real estate. Hence, domicile of the testator concerns movable property and not necessarily immoveable property, if it is located in a different state.

3.6 Where to keep the will after drafting

The safe deposit box is the most appropriate place if it can be opened without undue delay after the testator's death: alternatively, the will may be delivered to the executor or the Testator's lawyer or kept in a safe place with personal papers at home. In no event should a will be accessible to a 'disappointed heir'. Alternatively, a will can be registered by the testator at the sub-registrar's office, in which case a copy is kept there.

3.7 Language of the Will

A will may be written in any language and no technical words are necessary [(1909) ILR 36 Cal 149,156]. Only the wordings shall be such that the intention of the testator can be known therefrom [Section 74 of ISA 1925]. A Will may be written with any material ink or pencil. It may be partly in ink and partly in pencil.

3.8 Form of the Will

A Will may be in any form, but to be effective, it must be properly signed and attested as required by the Act. It is not necessary that it should be of a testamentary form in order to operate as a Will, but there must in all cases, be the *animus testandi* i.e. the intention that the writing should operate as a Will.

Declaration that this is the **last will** and previous wills are invalid

Declaration that the person is in good health and mind, and is making the will of their **own free choice**

Names of the **survivors** (wife and children etc.)

List of **moveable and immoveable property**

Description of **how the assets are to be divided**

Signature of the person with date

Names and Signatures of two witnesses

Figure: Illustration of the components of a will

A will may contain the following components (as a guideline):

- A declaration by the person that this is the last will and all previous wills are invalid

- A declaration that the person is in good health and mind, and is making the will of his own free choice

- Name of the survivors (wife and children)

- Description of the person's moveable and immoveable property

- How the assets are to be divided in in whose names

- Signature of the person with date

- Name and Signature of two witnesses

The figure above illustrates the components of a will.

3.9 Format of a sample will

The format of a sample will is as follows:

I, <name of testator>, son of <father's name>, aged <age in years>, resident of <address of testator>, declare this to be my last will and testament. This will cancels all my prior wills made by me.

I am in good health and possess a good mind. This will was made independently by me. No one has influenced or compelled me to make this will.

I hereby appoint <name of executor>, as the sole executor of this will.

My wife's name is <name of wife>. We have <number of children> children, whose names are as follows:

1.

2.

I have the following immovable and movable property:

1. A flat in the address _____

2. Jewelry, shares in various companies, cash and cash in bank accounts.

I declare that all the above assets are owned by me, and I have full authority over these assets.

I entrust all my movable and immovable properties to the following persons in the following ways

1. I give my bank account to my wife

2. I give my flat in the name of my son

(   )

Testator's signature

Date

Signed by the testator as a last will in our presence. We have fully understood and approved the material and have signed our names as witnesses in the presence of the testator and in the presence of each other.

Name and signature of witnesses:

1.

2.

3.10 Construction of Will [Section 74 of ISA 1925]

Wording of Will - It is not necessary that any technical words or terms of art be used in a Will but only that the wording be such that the intention of the testator can be known therefrom.

(i) In a court of construction, the only legitimate evidence of the testator's intention, is the will, itself, properly authenticated, and any codicil to it.

(ii) There are two cardinal principles to be observed in the construction of a Will, viz.

- the rule of law

- the rule of construction.

A rule of law is one which takes effect when certain conditions are found, although the testator may have intended to the contrary [Re Coward (1887) 57LT 285, AIR 1939 Cal 206]

A Rule of construction is one which points out what a court will do in the absence of express or implied intentions [1915 AC 207]

(iii) Another general principle which the court applies in the construction of Wills is that technical words or words of known legal import are to be considered as having been used in their technical sense, or according to their strict acceptance, unless the context contains a plain indication to the contrary [(1843) 6 MAW and G314, 342].

(iv). Intestacy is not to be likely inferred [Re Bailey (1951) Ch 407, 410].

(v) To ascertain the intention of the testator, the court is concerned with three distinct questions

- What words has the testator used to express the intention

- What is the meaning of such words in relation to the persons and things described

- What is the meaning of such words in relation to the disposition of such property among the donees.

When the intention of the testator has been discovered, the next enquiry by the court to ascertain whether there is any rule preventing the intention from taking effect and how the intention can be effectuated (Halisbury's Laws of England) .

3.11 Ambulatory character of a will

The essential quality of a testament is its ambulatoriness or its revocability during the testator's lifetime.

A "will", says Jarman, is an instrument by which a person makes a disposition of his property to take effect after his decease, and which is in its own nature ambulatory and revocable during his life.

The ambulatory character of the will has often been pointed out as its prominent characteristic, distinguishing it, in fact, from ordinary disposition by a living person's deed, which might indeed postpone the beneficial possession or even a vesting until the death of the disposer and yet would produce such postponement only by its express terms under an irrevocable instrument and a statement that a will is final does not import an agreement not to change it. A will is the aggregate of man's testamentary intentions so far as they are manifested in writing duly executed according to the statute.

A will or testament is a declaration in a prescribed manner of the intention of the person making it, with regard to the matters that he wishes to take effect upon or after his death (Halisbury's laws of England - 4th edition). The absence of a reference in the instrument that it shall come into effect after the lifetime was taken, under other circumstances, that it cannot be a will.

3.12 Advantages / importance of a will

A will allows a person to dispose of his property to the persons he selects, at the time he chooses, and in the amounts and proportions that he specifies. The person can also indicate how his property will be protected and who will be responsible for its protection. Anyone who is 21 years of age or above and mentally capable of understanding the nature of a will can have one drawn up. In some states or under some conditions, the age requirement can be reduced or waived.

3.13 Instructions and disposition

A letter of instruction may provide a lawyer or executor with essential information and simplify the task of carrying out the testator's desires. Such a letter is not part of the will, and need not comply with any formal requirements. Its purpose is to furnish a detailed inventory of the estate's assets, give instructions regarding the locations of all needed documents including birth, marriage, and military discharge records, ration card or social security card, insurance policies, a list of bank accounts and safe deposit boxes, title deeds, pension papers and so on, and summarize instructions regarding liquidation of business affairs.

Other portions of the letter may indicate where the will is kept.

3.14 Preparation and Execution of Wills

Some statutory formalities govern the preparation of all wills. For example, wills must be in writing, must demonstrate the testator's intent to pass property to heirs, and may as a rule incorporate another document or other documents existing when the will is drawn and if the will adequately identifies the additions. The only exceptions to the rule that wills must be written are "*nuncupative*" or "oral" wills. All wills have also to be signed, or given some visible mark intended as a signature at the end of the will in some states and in other places in other jurisdictions [Section 63(a) of ISA 1925].

Most states require that two witnesses attest to, or witness, the will's signatures [Section 63(c) of ISA 1925]. Some other states require three witnesses. Where statutes require it, wills have to be published, with the testator stating that the will is his or her own. Witnesses generally sign in the presence of testator and each other. No witness should be a beneficiary under the will. An attestation clause appearing before the witnesses' signature states that all formalities have been complied with, but is not mandatory. Such a clause merely serves as an evidence of proper execution.

Execution of a document is not a mere act of signing. The executor owns up recitals in the documents executed by him. He must, therefore, understand contents and terms of the documents before subscribing his signature [2000 (JV) CTC 490].

The will must be dated. If the will is not dated, proof of the date on which the will was executed is to be given at the time when the petition for probate is filed [Section 276 of ISA 1925].

3.16 Legal Status of Joint Wills and Mutual Wills

Joint wills (made by two persons in one document) and mutual wills (with reciprocal terms) are rare in India and may create complications. Courts often prefer separate wills for clarity.

3.17 Codicils and When to Use Them

A codicil is a document used to make minor amendments to an existing will. It must be signed and attested like a will. Use it when changes are not substantial enough to justify writing a new will.

3.18 Conclusion

With a foundational understanding of what constitutes a will and its key components, we must now look closely at the actual process involved in making a valid will. The subsequent chapter delves into the detailed procedures and precautions necessary to ensure that your will accurately reflects your wishes and stands firm legally.

Chapter 4: Making a Will

In this chapter, we go through some of the aspects of making a will.

4.1 Who can make a will

Every person who is not a minor or a man of unsound mind can make a will [Section 59 of Indian Succession Act 1925, which applies to all except Muslims]. By a man of "unsound mind" is meant not necessarily a lunatic, idiot or insane person but also a man, who though otherwise quite sane, is not at the moment of executing a deed, by reason of illness, in his proper senses and competent to understand what he is doing. It is necessary that he should be in a sound disposing condition, which means he must also be conscious of various claims persons have upon his property and must be capable of realizing the extent of the property disposed of under the will [AIR 1966 Allahabad 570].

Mere old age is no evidence of incapacity to make a will [A 1962 Patna 481]. When a will is made by a sick person, it is advisable to provide satisfactory evidence that the man is in his proper senses and able to understand what he declares. For this purpose it would be best, if practicable, to have the will attested by the medical attendant who may also append a certificate at the foot of the will that he has satisfied himself that the testator is in his proper senses. The will or any part of the will, the making of which is caused by fraud, coercion or such importunity as to take away the free agency of the testator will be void [Section 61 of ISA 1925].

4.2 How will is drafted / points to be considered before drafting a will

No particular form of will is prescribed by law, but the ordinary form in vogue in the country which has been followed for centuries may be easily adopted. The language employed should be as simple as possible and free from technical words and should be easily intelligible to a layman.

Before drafting a will, it is necessary to consider the following:

- Whether the testator is competent to draft a will

- Whether the property the testator wishes to bequeath is that which is legally bequeathable and which they are competent to bequeath

- Whether the devises are legally competent to take the devise.

- Whether the interest which the testator wishes to create can legally be created.

- Whether the conditions that the testator wishes to impose can legally be imposed

- Whether the machinery devised to be employed for carrying out his wishes is sufficient and legally sound

If the description as a whole or any part of a deed or document fails to ascertain the object of the writer or the parties and no meaning can be extracted, then the document or the clause must be rejected for uncertainty. Although a document which is vague or meaningless must be rejected, the courts often strive hard to construe them generously in order to make sense of them and give effect to them [see Odgers, Construction of deeds and statuettes, 5th Edition, pp 87-88].

4.3 How a will is made in India

Wills by all persons except Hindus, Buddhists, Sikhs, Jains and Muslims are governed by the Indian Succession Act 1925. The most important provisions of that act relating to wills, including those which relate to the form of the will, have however been applied to wills made by Hindus, Buddhists, Sikhs and Jains as well [Section 57 of ISA 1925].

The following formalities are prescribed by the Indian Succession Act for a will:

- The will should be made in writing except that a soldier or airman in active service or a mariner at sea, not being a Hindu, Buddhist, Sikh or Jain, can make an oral will [Section 63, 65 of ISA 1925].

- It should be signed or marked by the testator or by some other person in his presence and by his direction [Section 63(a) of ISA 1925]. The signature should be so placed that it should appear that it was intended thereby to give effect to the writing as a will [Section 63(b) of ISA 1925]. The best place is at the foot or end of the writing.

- It should be attested by two or more persons, each of whom have seen the testator making his signature or mark or has seen some other person signing the will in the presence and direction of the testator, or has received from the testator a personal acknowledgement of his signature or mark or the signature of some other person. Each of the attesting witnesses should sign the will in the presence of the testator, but it is not necessary that more than one witness should be present at the same time [Section 63(c) of ISA 1925]. In a case where the attesting witnesses' signatures appeared above the thumb mark of the testator, it was held that the attestation was invalid, as the witnesses appeared to have signed it even before the executant [(1998) 8 SCC 598].

4.4 Registration of a will

Registration of a will refers to the process where the will is registered by the testator at the office of the sub-registrar. While registering the will, the testator must submit his identity proof, address proof and photograph and those of his witnesses, who accompany the testator to the sub-registrar's office. The advantage of registering is that the will is kept in the safe custody of the registrar and hence, cannot be tampered with. A registered will can also be withdrawn or overridden by a newer one.

There are a few points that must be kept in mind regarding registration:

(a) The registration of a will is optional [Section 18 of ISA 1925], [A 1962 SC 567]. There are special provisions in part IX of the Registration Act, under which a testator may deposit his will in a sealed cover with the Registrar. On the death of the testator, any person can apply to have the will opened and copied in the Register. The court can also require the production of such a will from the Registrar, who will open it and send it to the court after copying it out in his Register.

(b) The mere fact that a will is not registered does not make it improbable, much less impossible, that the will was executed [AIR 1954 SC 280]. The supreme court has held categorically that to draw an adverse inference against a will's genuineness if not registered is not warranted by law.

(c) Effect of registration of a will: Just a non-registration cannot constitute an inference against the genuineness of a will, mere registration does not dispel the requirement of proof of the will [AIR 1995 KER 208]. Its genuineness cannot be presumed [(1999) 2 Mad LJ 634/DB].

(d) Registration will not be taken as explaining away suspicion. Non-registration is also not a suspicious circumstance [AIR 2009 NOC 274], [2005 All LJ 1062].

4.5 Corrections to a will

All obliterations, interlineation and other alterations made in the will must be executed in the same way as the will, i.e. it must be signed by the testator and attested by witnesses [Section 71 of ISA 1925]. This can be done if there are one or two alterations by the testator and witnesses signing on the margin opposite the alterations, but if there are several alterations, it should be more convenient to make a memorandum at the end.

4.6 Mistakes Commonly Made When Drafting Wills

Common errors include ambiguous wording, failing to appoint an executor, omitting digital assets, or using witnesses who are also beneficiaries. These can invalidate the will. So it is important for the testator to be aware of such common mistakes.

4.7 Use of Templates and Do-It-Yourself Wills

While basic templates are available, DIY wills (such as those available and downloadable freely or at a low cost from the internet) should be approached with caution. Mistakes in format, attestation, or unclear phrasing can lead to probate issues. Legal review is advisable.

4.8 Conclusion

Now that we comprehend the step-by-step process of drafting and registering a valid will, the next critical aspect is discerning the intent behind the testator's decisions. The following chapter will guide us through understanding how courts interpret the true intentions of a testator, a crucial factor in upholding the validity of any will.

Chapter 5: Intention of the Testator

In this chapter, we discuss an important aspect of a will: how to determine the real intention of the testator or the person making the will.

5.1 Who is a Testator?

Testator is a deceased person who has left a valid will or codicil. In modern usage, a person who leaves a will is called testator.

Testatrix is the name given to a female testator

5.2 Intention: Dictionary meaning (according to Halisbury law)

Intention has been defined as the fixed direction of mind to a particular object or the determination to act in a particular manner. It is distinguishable from motive which incites of stimulates action. A man's intention ought to be judged by his acts and not what may be in his mind. It should be ascertained by taking into consideration the entire transaction [Ragubir Singh v Commissioner of Income Tax – AIR 1958 Punjab 250].

Intention is the purpose or design with which an act is done. It is the foreknowledge of the act, coupled with the desire of it, such foreknowledge and desire being the cause of the act, in as much as they fulfil themselves through the operation of the will [John Salmond, Jurisprudence p 378].

A testamentary document requires no special form of words. A will may be made in any form and in any language. This section lays down that no technical words or terms of art are required to be used in making a will. But if technical words are used by the testator, he will be presumed to use them in their legal sense unless the context indicates a clear contrary intention [Thillusion v Wordfall – 4 Vis 329]

When a testator has executed a will in some form, one must assume that he did not intend to make it a solemn farce – that he did not intend to die intestate when he has gone through the form of making a will. One ought if possible to read the will so as to lead to a testacy not an intestacy. This is the golden rule [Theobald on Wills 14th Edition p189].

There are two cardinal principles to be observed in the construction of the wills viz. the rule of law and the rule of construction. A rule of construction is one which points out what a court will do in the absence of express or implied intention. A rule of law is one which takes effect when certain conditions are found, although the testator may have intended to the contrary [Re Concord (1887) S7 LT 285].

5.3 What is the intention of a testator?

In determining the construction of a will, what we must look into is the intention of the testator. The Hindu law, no less than the English law, points to the intention as the element by which we are to be guided in determining the effect of testamentary disposition; nor is there any difference between one law and the other as to the materials from which the intention has to be collected. Primarily the words of the will are to be considered. They convey the expression of the testator's wishes, but the meaning to be attached to these may be affected by surrounding circumstances and where this is the case, the circumstances no doubt must be regarded [Lakshmanan v R. Ramier (1953) 4 SCR 848].

The testator's intention shown by the will cannot be varied according to the actual course of subsequent events [Halisbury's law]. Repeating the observations of Lord Moulton, Mukherjee J observes in [Jaba vs Jitendra, AIR 1949, PC 64] –

"All authorities agree that in a will the cardinal rule to be observed is to ascertain the real intention of the testator, which the will itself by express words or by implication declares. The primary duty of the court is to ascertain from the language of the entire document what the intentions of the testator are. The point must consider the surrounding circumstances, the position of the testator, his family relationship, the probability that he would use words in a particular sense and many other things which are often summed up in the somewhat picturesque figure, the court is entitled to put itself in the testator's armchair.

To ascertain the intention of the testator, the court is concerned with three distinct questions:

- What words has the testator used to express his intention

- What is the meaning of such words in relation to the persons and the things described; and

- What is the meaning of the words in relation to the disposition of such property among the donee(s)

When the intention of the testator has been discovered, the next enquiry by the court should be to ascertain whether there is any rule preventing the intention from taking effect and how the intention can be effectuated (Halisbury law).

5.4 Testator's intention

The primary duty of the court is to endeavor to ascertain the intention of the testator from the will itself by reading it as a whole, without indulging in any conjecture or speculation on what the testator would have done if he had been better informed or better advised and from the language used by him, and in doing so the court is entitled and bound to bear in mind other matters than merely the words used in the will [AIR 1945 PC 113, AIR 1991 Kant 86].

The court should ensure that the testator's intention is to be effectuated as far as possible [Section 87 of ISA 1925]. The intention of the testator shall not be set aside because it cannot take effect to the full extent, but effect has to be given to it as far as possible.

The construction of the will is, in the first place considered quite apart from the question of the legality of the provisions of the will. For the purpose of ascertaining the intention, the will is to be read as whole, without references to the consequence if any rule of law is transgressed

[AIR 1977 MAD 87]. Once the intention is collected, the rule of law should be applied to ascertain if the court can carry out the intention wholly or in part.

In all cases, the primary duty of the court is to ascertain from the language of the testator what were his intentions, i.e. to construe the will. It is true in doing so they are entitled and bound to bear in mind other matters than merely the words used. They must consider the surrounding circumstances. Among such surrounding circumstances, which the court is bound to consider, none would be more important than race and religious opinions and the court is bound to regard them as presumably present in the mind of the testator, influences and aims arising therefrom. The court is justified in refusing to allow defects in expression in these matters to prevent the carrying out of the testator's true intentions. However, the intentions must be ascertained by the proper construction of the words he uses, and once ascertained, they must not be departed from [AIR 1935 Cal 716].

It is a well settled rule of construction that the same words used in a document (will) are to be given the same meaning until there is a clear intention to the contrary [AIR 1965 SC 1730]. Clear and unambiguous dispositive words are not to be controlled or qualified by any general expression of intention [AIR 1932 Cal 600].

At the same time, it must be recognized that documents in the vernacular are often expressed in loose and incorrect language and thus sometimes a meaning has to be given to particular words in vernacular documents, provided the context justifies in doing so [AIR 1930 PC 242]. Particular words in a will should not be constructed with reference to similar words in another will. The will must be read as a whole to ascertain the intention of the testator and where the intention is clearly expressed by unambiguous words in certain clauses, other words in other clauses repugnant to them must be discarded [AIR 1936 Pat 323].

5.5 Holographic will

A holographic will is a will which is written by the testator himself. A holograph will may show indication that the testator was fully conscious of what he was doing and will not be easily set aside [AIR 1929 Cal 290 / AIR 1960 Cal 551].

In the case of a holographic will, there is a presumption in favor of genuineness for the very good reason that the mind of the testator in physically writing out his own will is more apparent. When the testator says that he signed the will in the presence of attestors and attestors have signed in his presence and in the presence of each other, it raises a strong presumption of regularity in the execution and attestation [AIR 1964 SC 529].

Denoting a document wholly in the handwriting of the person whose signature it bears, the law makes a great presumption of genuineness in favor of a holographic will. A holographic will may show indication that the testator was fully conscious of what he was doing and will not be easily set aside and that what he did was an act of his own volition especially when he called entirely independent and responsible persons to be the witness of his will.

The court held that a greater degree of presumption arises in the case of holographic wills. The said finding was arrived at as the writing of the will and the signature of the testator was admitted; there was also due and proper attestation in accordance with the relevant statutory provisions. The court held no suspicious circumstances appeared on the face of the instrument and it was found moderate and rational [AIR 2009 SC 1389].

To apply the test of high probative value of a holograph will, it must first be pleaded and proved that it was in the handwriting of the testator. It had also the benefit of a handwriting expert to express an opinion that the handwriting appearing in the will was identical with those of the testator appearing from other admitted documents produced by the adversary himself. In case of a holographic will, the presumption of genuineness is all the more even bordering on actual proof of due execution and attestation of the will [(1996) 8 SCC 124].

A will that is handwritten by the testator. Such a will is typically unattested. Holographic wills are rooted in the civil law tradition. A holographic will is a will which is in the handwriting of the person who has executed it and signed by him. It is necessary that the entire will should be in the writing of the testator. A holographic will can revoke a former will executed earlier, just as an ordinary will.

The holographic will must be entirely in their own handwriting including the signature which needs to be proved by witnesses familiar with them during probate of the will. A holographic will is purely stating that it must be made in accordance with the appropriate state laws and is subject to prescribed conditions and limitations. The principal requirement is that it must be entirely in the testator's own handwriting.

5.6 Suspicious Circumstances surrounding a will

Some examples of what might or might not be held as suspicious circumstances are as follows:

- Even a delay in registration was held not sufficient to discredit the genuineness of the will [AIR 2000 Ori 10].

- Law does not stand in the way of a man disposing of his self-acquired property in the way he likes. That is the very purport of the will, but at the same time when a person who is a natural heir is disinherited, he is entitled to know why he has been disinherited [AIR 1990 SC 1742].

- In a case in Pramilla Sundari v Bijoy Ghosal [(2000) 11 CHN 754] the bench of Calcutta high court inferred the suspicious circumstances from the elucidation of several factors relating to the positions of the signatures of the testator and the witnesses such as:

- A literate testator affixing a thumb impression is itself a suspicious circumstance [AIR 1998 MP 46].

- Inimical disposition of the beneficiary to the testator would definitely excite the suspicion of the court [AIR 1995 SC 101].

- Incorrect statements in the will with regards to existence or non-existence of a relative will also be a suspicious circumstance [(1992) 2 JT 125].

- Non mention of a date, want of signature of the testator beneath the operative part of the will, non-examination of both witnesses were considered to be suspicious [(1991) DLT 6].

In sum, a circumstance would be suspicious when it is not normal or it is not normally expected in a normal situation or it is not expected of a normal person [AIR 1982 SC 133]

5.7 Other Suspicious Circumstances

Children awarded different amounts and not giving any money to widowed daughter is not an unnatural thing [AIR 2002 SC 317].

Rule of Barry v. Butlin: Which lays down that the onus probandi is always on the person who propounds the will and the person that takes a benefit excites the suspicion of court which must be dispelled by evidence that supports the instrument.

If the beneficiaries under the will had taken an active part in the execution, that by itself is not sufficient to create any doubt either about testamentary capacity or genuineness of the will [AIR 1987 SC 767].

The will has not been produced for very many years before the court of public authorities even though there were occasions to produce it for plaintiffs title to property. The will was rejected as not genuine [AIR 1990 SC 396].

If there are unexplained circumstances then inquitious disposition and untrue statements in the will would create suspicious circumstances, otherwise not [AIR1976 Cal 377].

In the case of suspicion against the will, the court will see the intention of the testator in disposing his property which is of paramount importance. The first question to be considered is whether the dispositions in the will are natural, fair, reasonable and probate. This goes a long way in effecting the theory or vitiating suspicious circumstances.

The suspicious circumstances may be as to the genuineness of the signatures of the testator, the condition of the testator's mind, the disposition made in the will being unnatural, improper unfair in the light of relevant circumstances, or there might be other indicators in the will to show that the testator's mind was not free.

If the probator himself takes a predominant part in the execution of the will which confers a substantial benefit on him then that is also a circumstance to be taken into account.

Any and every circumstance is not a 'suspicious' circumstance and would be 'suspicious' when it is not normal or is not normally expected in a normal situation or is not expected of a normal person. To be valid, a will must be signed by the testator. The signature must be intended by the testator as an act of execution and it must appear that he intended by the signature to give effect to his will.

Where various discrepancies establish a number of suspicious circumstances surrounding the execution of the will that justifies a reasonable conclusion that the will was obtained in collusion with one or two members to defeat the claims of others, and that the propounder failed to satisfy the conscience of the court regarding the execution and attestation of the will [AIR 1973 Cal 460] as in the case of proof of other documents so in the case of wills, it would be idle to expect proof with mathematical certainty. The test to be applied would be the usual test of satisfaction of a prudent person in such matters [AIR 1972 Pat 146].

Delay in publishing a will, when an occasion presented itself to make it known even earlier would be a suspicious circumstance [AIR 1990 SC 396, AIR 1992 SC 1414].

Failure to state why the persons who are otherwise legally entitled to inherit, are disinherited in the will is a suspicious circumstance [AIR 1990 SC 396].

Sometimes a combination of several factors like, cancellation of an earlier will, no 'kieral' on each page, propounder taking active part, disinheritance of daughter and undue preference shown to son, poor state of health of testatrix, registration officer overlooking patent defects in the will, death of testatrix the day following execution may be so telling on suspicious character of the document [1998 2 MLJ 307].

In another case inexplicable gaps, non-mention of earlier will, stipulation that propounder would be responsible for cremation expenses and presence of strangers as attesting witnesses constituted unedifying factors to betray the falsity of the will [AIR 1999 MP 240].

Inimical disposition of the beneficiary to the testator would definitely excite the suspicion of the court [AIR 1995 SC 1010]. Incorrect statements in the will with regard to existence or non-existence of a relative will also be a suspicious circumstance [1992 2 SCC 507].

The fact that the earlier wills executed by the testator had not been set out in the last will would not by itself be treated as a suspicious circumstance [AIR 1995 SC 2086].

Will executed under suspicious circumstance – to prove the genuineness of the will, the propounder has to prove five things:

- The testamentary capacity of the testator

- The testamentary nature of the instrument that is, that the document does not dispose of any property in present but only on the death of the executant

- The testator's knowledge of the contents of the instrument and his approval of the same

- The absence of undue influence, fraud etc

- Due execution by the testator and its attestation by witnesses as required by law

List of Suspicious circumstances:

- Signature of the testator may be very shaky and doubtful

- The condition of the testator's mind may appear to be very feeble and debilitated

- Mental capacity of the testator

- The dispositions made in the will may appear to be unnatural, improbable or unfair

- The will may otherwise indicate that the said dispositions may not be the result of the testator's free will of mind

- Caveat show exercise of undue influence, fraud or coercion in respect of execution of will

- Propounder themselves takes a prominent part in the execution of the will which confers on them substantial benefit.

5.8 Conclusion

Recognizing the importance of clearly capturing the testator's intention, we turn our attention next to the probate process, a crucial judicial step to enforce the terms of a will.

Chapter 6: Wills Under Personal Laws in India

In India, the law governing wills is not entirely uniform. While the Indian Succession Act, 1925 is the principal legislation regulating wills and succession for most Indians, certain religious communities are governed by their own personal laws, which may differ significantly in both substance and procedure. It is essential for anyone drafting, executing, or contesting a will to understand these differences to avoid costly mistakes and future disputes.

6.1 The General Rule: Indian Succession Act, 1925

For most Indian citizens—including Hindus, Buddhists, Sikhs, Jains, Christians, and Parsis—the Indian Succession Act, 1925 lays down the rules for testamentary succession, that is, succession according to a will. However, there are notable exceptions and modifications for certain religious communities, particularly Muslims, and in some cases Parsis and Christians in specific regions.

6.2 Hindu, Buddhist, Sikh, and Jain Law

Historically, Hindu law did not recognize wills; the concept was introduced during British rule and was later codified. Today, the Indian Succession Act governs wills made by Hindus, Buddhists, Sikhs, and Jains, except in cases where special customs or regional laws apply.

Key features of Hindu law related to succession include:

- Freedom of disposition: Hindus, Buddhists, Sikhs, and Jains can freely dispose of their self-acquired property by will, subject to certain restrictions if the property is ancestral or joint family property.

- No restrictions on bequest: There is no statutory limit on how much property can be bequeathed, or to whom, as long as the testator has the legal capacity.

- Applicability of the Act: Sections 57 to 191 of the Indian Succession Act apply.

Points to note:

- Ancestral property, if governed by Mitakshara law, may have limitations on disposition without consent of coparceners.

- Customs or state amendments may create further exceptions.

6.3 Muslim Law

For Muslims in India, testamentary succession is governed by Muslim Personal Law (Shariat), not the Indian Succession Act, except where the marriage is solemnized under the Special Marriage Act.

Key features for succession as per Muslim Personal Law include the following:

- Bequest limit: A Muslim can only will away up to one-third of their estate (after payment of funeral expenses and debts) to non-heirs, unless the other heirs consent to a greater bequest.

- Restrictions: Bequests to heirs (those who are already entitled to a share under Muslim law) are generally invalid without consent of the other heirs.

- Oral wills: Oral (nuncupative) wills are recognized if proved satisfactorily, especially if made during illness (marz-ul-maut).

- No requirement for attestation or registration: There is no requirement that a Muslim will be in writing, attested, or registered, though a written and witnessed will is always preferable for evidentiary reasons.

Its practical implications include the following:

- If a Muslim testator wills away more than one-third of their property to a non-heir, the will is only valid to that extent unless all legal heirs consent to the larger disposition after the testator's death.

- If the will is challenged, courts look for clear evidence of the testator's intention and compliance with Shariat requirements.

6.4 Christian and Parsi Law

Christians

For Indian Christians, the Indian Succession Act applies to wills, but Part VI (Sections 59–191) of the Act, which deals with testamentary succession, is specifically applicable. Some state amendments or regional laws may provide minor variations.

- No statutory restrictions on the amount or kind of property that can be bequeathed.

- Formality requirements: Written wills must be signed and attested by two witnesses, as per the Act.

Parsis

Parsis are governed by special provisions within the Indian Succession Act (Sections 50–56), but broadly, the testamentary freedom is similar to that of other communities governed by the Act.

- Widow's right: Certain rules ensure that a widow cannot be entirely disinherited.

- Attestation and formality: Similar to other Indian citizens, wills must be in writing and properly attested.

6.5 Special Cases: Interfaith Marriages and Special Marriage Act

Where a marriage is solemnized under the Special Marriage Act, 1954, the parties and their descendants are generally governed by the Indian

Succession Act, irrespective of their religion. This can override personal law restrictions.

Example: A Muslim who marries under the Special Marriage Act may, for the purposes of wills and succession, be governed by the Indian Succession Act rather than Muslim Personal Law.

6.6 Table: Applicability of Succession Law by Community

Community	Governing Law for Wills	Key Restrictions/Notes
Hindu, Buddhist, Sikh, Jain	Indian Succession Act, 1925	Free disposition, some custom-based exceptions
Muslim	Muslim Personal Law (Shariat)	Max 1/3rd to non-heir without heirs' consent
Christian	Indian Succession Act, 1925	No significant statutory restrictions
Parsi	Indian Succession Act, 1925 (Particular Provisions)	Some protection for widow, otherwise free
Interfaith (Special Marriage Act)	Indian Succession Act, 1925	Overrides personal law for succession/wills

6.7 Practical Tips for Will-Making Under Personal Laws

- **Always check which law applies:** The testator's religion, the form of marriage, and state of residence can all affect which law governs the will.

- **Respect religious restrictions:** Especially for Muslims, exceeding the allowed bequest limit without heirs' consent can invalidate a will's provisions.

- **Record consents where necessary:** Where heirs' consent is required, it should be recorded in writing to prevent disputes.

- **Consult a specialist:** When in doubt, consult a lawyer familiar with the relevant personal law before drafting or executing a will.

6.8 Conclusion

India's diversity of personal laws means that the drafting and execution of wills is not a "one-size-fits-all" matter. Understanding the interplay between the Indian Succession Act and various religious personal laws is essential to ensure that a will is valid, enforceable, and truly reflects the testator's intentions. A little attention to these details can prevent future litigation and ensure peace among heirs.

Chapter 7: International Aspects and Cross-Border Succession

In our increasingly globalized world, it is common for Indian citizens to own assets abroad, have family members living overseas, or even reside outside India themselves. This growing cross-border reality brings fresh challenges to will-making and succession planning. Understanding how international laws interact with Indian law is crucial to ensure that a person's wishes are honoured without unnecessary legal hurdles or costly litigation.

7.1 Why International Succession Matters

International or cross-border succession arises in many scenarios, such as:

- An Indian resident owns property or bank accounts in a foreign country.

- A Non-Resident Indian (NRI) wishes to distribute Indian and foreign assets.

- An heir or beneficiary lives outside India.

- A will is executed in one country but needs to be enforced in another.

In such cases, the succession process can be complicated by differences in local laws, conflict of laws rules, and practical issues like documentation and probate.

7.2 Basic Principles: Which Law Applies?

The main questions in cross-border succession are:

- Which country's law determines the validity of the will?

- Which law governs the inheritance of movable (personal) and immovable (real) property?

The general rules are as follows:

- Movable property (e.g., bank accounts, shares, jewellery): Usually governed by the law of the deceased's domicile at the time of death.

- Immovable property (e.g., land, buildings): Governed by the law of the country where the property is located (lex situs).

Domicile refers to a person's permanent home, not just their country of residence.

7.3 Indian Law on Foreign Assets and Wills

- Indian law generally recognizes that assets situated outside India will be governed by the law of the country where the assets are located.

- If an Indian testator makes a will for foreign property, that will should comply with the law of the foreign jurisdiction for the will to be valid and effective in that country.

- It is possible to have a separate will for assets in each country or to create a single will covering all assets, but this must be carefully drafted to avoid accidental revocation of either will.

Practical tip:

If you have substantial assets in another country, consider preparing a separate will in accordance with the local laws of that country and clearly state in each will which assets it covers.

7.4 Recognition of Indian Wills Abroad

Whether a will made in India is recognized in another country depends on the following:

- The formal requirements of that country (e.g., attestation, registration, notarization).

- Whether the foreign court recognizes Indian probate.

- If the will is in English, many countries (e.g., UK, Australia) are more likely to accept it if other formalities are met.

Probate process:

- Some countries require an Indian will to be probated in India before it is enforced there.

- After probate, the executor or heir may need to apply for "re-sealing" or "ancillary probate" in the foreign jurisdiction.

7.5 Enforcement of Foreign Wills in India

If a will is executed outside India and assets are located within India:

- The will must comply with the Indian Succession Act and local formalities for it to be valid in India.

- The executor or heir may need to apply for probate or letters of administration in an Indian court.

- If the will has been probated by a court in the UK, Singapore, Hong Kong, or certain other "notified" countries (as per the Indian Succession Act), an application can be made to the relevant High Court in India to "re-seal" the probate, making it effective in India.

List of notified countries (subject to updates): UK, Australia, New Zealand, Canada, Hong Kong, Singapore, Malaysia, among others.

7.6 Double Taxation and Inheritance Tax

Cross-border succession may raise taxation issues such as the following:

- India currently does not have inheritance tax, but several countries (such as the UK, USA, France, Japan) do.

- An Indian heir inheriting assets abroad may have to pay local inheritance or estate taxes.

- Double taxation treaties (DTAAs) sometimes provide relief, but careful planning is required.

7.7 Common Challenges in Cross-Border Succession

Some common challenges that are encountered when the succession is across borders includes the following:

- Multiple probates: Separate court procedures may be needed in each country where the deceased held property.

- Language and documentation: Certified translations and apostilled/legalized documents may be required.

- Conflict of laws: Laws regarding forced heirship, legitimacy, and marital rights may differ significantly by country.

- Delay and expense: International succession can be time-consuming and costly without advance planning.

7.8 Practical Steps for NRIs and Persons with Global Assets

Some practical steps that an NRI or a person with global assets with links with India can take are as follows:

- Take inventory: List all assets in India and abroad, with clear ownership details.

- Decide on will structure: Consider separate wills for different jurisdictions or a carefully drafted worldwide will (with clear exclusions to prevent accidental revocation).

- Consult experts: Use legal counsel familiar with succession laws of each country involved.

- Fulfil formalities: Ensure each will meets the formal and substantive requirements of the applicable country (witnesses, attestation, etc.).

- Consider digital assets: Include instructions for digital or cryptocurrency assets, if any, especially if located on international platforms.

- Update regularly: Revise your will if you move countries or acquire new assets abroad.

7.9 Sample Scenarios

Some sample scenarios for illustration are provided below:

Example 1: Indian Resident with Property in the UK
Mr. Sharma, an Indian citizen domiciled in Delhi, owns a flat in London and a house in Mumbai. He can make two wills—one in India for Indian assets, another in the UK for the London property. Each will should state that it only covers assets in that country.

Example 2: NRI Settled in the USA with Parents in India
Ms. Patel, an NRI in New York, inherits property from her parents in Gujarat. To transfer the property, she must obtain Indian probate or letters of administration, and follow US reporting requirements for inheritance.

Example 3: Foreign Will Covering Indian Assets
A US citizen executes a will in California covering all assets, including a plot in Goa. To transfer the Goan property, the executor must get the will probated in India, ensuring the will complies with Indian law.

7.10 Conclusion

International and cross-border succession require careful planning, attention to detail, and awareness of both Indian and foreign laws. The key is to avoid "one-size-fits-all" solutions and seek professional advice. A well-drafted succession plan ensures that global assets are smoothly transferred, disputes are minimized, and the testator's wishes are fulfilled without unnecessary delay or litigation.

Chapter 8: Probate of a Will

In this chapter, we discuss the concept of probate and the steps needed for a heir or executor to file a petition for probate of a will in Indian courts.

8.1 Introduction to Probate

Probate is the legal procedure in which the deceased person's property is examined and evaluated, claims against the estate are paid and the remaining property is distributed:

- to the heirs if there is a will or

- according to intestacy / state law if no will

Probate is also the name given to the petition to the court for granting the authority to an executor to execute the will of a testator.

Probate of a will, when granted, establishes the will from the death of the testator and renders valid all intermediate acts of the executor as such.

As the executor derives his title under the will and all the properties of the testator vest in him immediately on the death of the testator, on the grant of probate, all his intermediate acts in connection with the estate are validated [AIR 1956 Mod 274]. This section enacts that the vesting takes place on the taking of probate but relates back to the time of the testator's death and to the estate which then belonged to him. Under Section 221 of ISA 1925, in the case of an administrator only those acts which are beneficial to the estate and validated by the grant are validated.

Probate and letters of administration with a copy of the will annexed are conclusive evidence of the testamentary capacity of the testator, as to the factum of its due execution and validity of the will [AIR 1959 Cal 795] and the finding of the probate court as to the due execution of the will is conclusive [AIR 1992 Mad 136].

Probate is conclusive as to the genuineness of the will and appointment of executors.

Once probate is granted, no suit will lie for a declaration that the testator was not of a sound mind.

Probate is conclusive as to the representative title of the executor against the debtors of the deceased and gives complete indemnity to them, as per Section 273 of ISA 1925.

The moment the probate is granted, it will relate back from the date of death of the testator and all property will be vested in the person in whose favor the probate was granted. The probate decides only the validity of the will and has no bearing to the title to the property itself, of whether the testator owned the property and whether the property stood validly transferred to a person claiming under a will [2003 7 SC 301].

8.2 Court procedure for probate

The court procedure for probating a will generally include the following steps:

- **Submission**: Petitioners submit probate application at the court in the prescribed format, along with death certificate, affidavit and court fees

- **Verification**: Court receives the probate application and verifies details

- **Publication**: Court directs to publish in newspapers a notice inviting members of the public and next of kin to file objections. It also directs to send notification letters to the next of kin

- **Issuance**: If there is no objection, the court issues the probate and letters of administration

- **Upon Objection**: If there is an objection, the normal court procedure takes place. After examining evidence and arguments, the court issues its judgment regarding the grant of probate.

8.3 Functions of a probate court

[Section 227 of Indian Succession Act 1925]

The functions of a probate court are:

- To see that the will has been actually executed by the testator in a sound disposing state of mind without coercion or undue influence

- That it has been duly attested

- To determine whether the document is of the testamentary character and whether the person applying for the probate is entitled to be constituted the legal representative of the deceased

- Its primary function is to deal with the factum and due execution of the will

- If the court comes to the conclusion that a part of the document only and not the whole of it is a result of the testator's act or has been executed under influence, the probate court excludes from the grant of those portions.

- However, the probate court is not entitled to exclude any portion of the propounded document from probate on a ground which requires the decision of the probate court on a point of construction or on a point which touches the validity of the bequest contained in the will [AIR 1940 2 Cal 458].

- It is also not competent for the probate court to determine whether the testator had or had not the power to dispose of the property which he purports to dispose of by his will. [AIR 2000 KER 241]

- Where there is a contest between two rival wills, the question before the court is: which of those is the last will of the testator. Only on the finding of the said issue, the question of grant of probate validates all intermediate acts by the executor [AIR 1992 MP 224]

- The question whether the probate court can go into other matters while deciding the question of granting probate came in consideration in Ramachandra v Sarja Bajrao [AIR 1985 Bom 113], wherein it was held that the probate when granted establishes the will from the death of the testatrix.

- The court will only construe the will to find out if the person propounding the will is appointed executor, either expressly or by implication, and whether the document is a will [(1893) ILR 20 Cal 885].

- All the high courts have consistently held that it is not the function of the probate court to determine the question of title. The earliest case is Behari Lal v Jaggo [(1879) ILR Cal 1].

- In Kashi Ram v Gobind Lal [(1949) 2 Cal 88] it was observed that the view taken in Behari Lal's case has been followed by the high courts of Calcutta, Bombay, Madras, Allahabad and Patna.

- In Chand Mal v Lachi Narain [(1900) ILR 22 Allahabad 662] it was held that the whole document and not only a part of it should be admitted to probate and the same view has been taken by the Calcutta High Court [(1949) 2 Cal 418].

- The probate court is not a court of construction. In Bai Parekh v Raghunath [42 Bom LR 1063] court said that it is not the province of the testamentary judge to determine whether the property covered by the will or for which letter of administration were asked for, was the property of the deceased or not or whether it was the joint property belonging to the deceased and someone else.

- Probate court should not decide who are the persons beneficially interested in the estate. The question whether the bequest is good or bad is also not within the purview of the probate court

- Probate court does not decide any question of will or existence of the property itself. [AIR 1954 SC 280, AIR 1970 Assam 111]

8.4 Jurisdiction of the probate court

- The probate court has no jurisdiction to go into the question of the validity of the provision of the will [AIR 1936 Leh 378].

- If the document propounded for probate is not a will, i.e. it is not a document of testamentary character, the probate court has no jurisdiction to grant probate of such a document.

- Scope of probate: In the Supreme Court of India – AIR 1954 SC 280/252/1953 Iswar Narain Singh v Kamla Devi, F/B/Three judged the scope as follows: Court of probate has no jurisdiction to decide if a particular bequest is good or bad. The court of probate is only concerned with the question as to whether the document put forward as the last will and testament of a deceased person was duly executed and attested in accordance with the law and whether at the time of each execution, the testator had a sound disposing mind.

- Jurisdiction of the district judge to grant probate: The matter of Ugar Chand v Surajmal [2 Bom LR 605] deals with the instance of whether the deceased had a fixed place of abode within the jurisdiction of the district judge. The expression 'had a fixed place of abode' used in the section is equivalent to reside and the word 'reside' or 'residence' denotes the place where an individual eats, drinks, and sleeps, or where his family or servants eat, drink and sleep [AIR 1923 Nag 145].

- The jurisdiction of the probate or letters of administration is a special jurisdiction – not called upon to adjudicate the title of the property dealt in a will. Also, it confines to the legality, genuineness and such other matters regarding the will as are sought to be proved.

8.5 Probate only to the appointed executor, and of what instrument probate cannot be granted

- Probate can only be granted to an executor appointed by the will expressly or in accordance with the law [AIR 1977 Del 34] [Section 222 of ISA 1925]

- When there are more than one executors, probate must be granted to all who apply, as per Section 224 of ISA 1925.

- The court does not have discretion to refuse probate on the ground that in its opinion the applicant is not fit to be appointed as executor

- The will which simply appoints a testamentary guardian ought not to be admitted to probate [1958, Allahabad 832]

- If a will is limited to a foreign country, it is not entitled to probate in this country.

- A writing which is not of a testamentary character is not entitled to probate

- If one part of an instrument operates in present as a deed and another in future as a will, probate may be granted of the later portion [(1900) ILR 22 Allahabad 162]

- Marginal notes and alterations made by the testator in his will which are unattested cannot be admitted to probate [15 Bom LR 352].

- Probate may be granted of part of the will and other parts omitted if these other parts are not proved to have been prepared under the instruction of the testator. [(1910) 12 Bom LR 569]

- A probate cannot be granted to a person who is a minor, or is of unsound mind.

8.6 Probate of a part of a will [ISA 4th Edition 1978, Sanjiba Row]

There is no provision in the act which authorizes the court to grant probate restricted to a part of an estate while the whole estate is vested in the executor. But a will may be admitted in part to probate and probate may be refused in regards the other part, as for instance where the court is satisfied that there has been an insertion in the will of a clause by fraud or without the knowledge of the testator or by forgery after his death. In any such case, probate is granted only in respect to that portion of the will which is not validated by any such circumstances [AIR 1925 PC45].

It is clear that the court is not entirely without jurisdiction to make a grant of letters of authorization with the will annexed, limited to part only of an estate, Section 255 to Section 257 of the ISA 1925 recognize sufficiently that there is jurisdiction in the court to appropriate case to limit the grant to part of an estate alone [AIR 1955 Mad 411, AIR 1975 Mad 342].

8.7 Selecting an executor

Selecting the person who will oversee the distribution of one's estate according to one's will is as important as choosing a trustee. The loyalty and ability of the executor may be the single most critical factor in ensuring effective and fair administration of one's assets after one's death: particularly in preventing losses and protecting the property one has left under his will.

Subject to the supervision of an appropriate court, the executor takes possession of the assets specified in the will, manages the estate as the deceased would have, pays debts, taxes and expenses, retains legal counsel as required, and through counsel handles all the legal obligations and procedures incident to the "execution" of the will. The executor also accounts to the court and heirs for his or her stewardship and distributes the estate's assets according to the provision of the will and applicable legal strictures. Business skill and judgement, diligence and the capacity to attend to details and maintain proper records are essential qualities of good executors.

Executors fees are based on the size of the estate, but typically range from 1 or 1.5 percent to 2.5 percent of the gross estate.

8.8 Time Limits and Jurisdiction for Filing Probate Petitions

There is no fixed limitation period under Indian law, but undue delay may raise suspicion. Probate petitions must be filed in the jurisdiction where the deceased resided or where the assets are located.

8.9 Delays and Complications in Probate Proceedings

Delays in probate often arise due to legal objections, unclear asset titles, or missing documents. Engaging a probate lawyer early can help pre-empt challenges and streamline the process.

8.10 Conclusion

Having explored the concept of probate and its importance in giving legal effect to a will, it becomes imperative to understand how to initiate and manage probate proceedings in court. The next chapter addresses precisely that, explaining how a petition for probate is prepared, filed, and processed within India's judicial framework.

Chapter 9: Petition for Probate

In this chapter, we discuss in more detail about the components of a probate petition filed in the courts.

9.1 The Limitation Act

The Limitation Act does not deal with the enforcement of a right under a will and article 137 of the Limitation Act has no application in probate proceedings or the application for probate [AIR 1991 MP 11 / AIR 1987 PSH 126]. Supreme Court made a general observation that Article 137 of the Limitation Act can be applied to any petition under any act. It was held that the application for probate is in the nature of an application for permission to perform a duty acted by a will or for recognition as a testamentary trustee. MP High Court has also taken a similar view when cited in Shobha Vs Janki [AIR 1987 MP 145] where all the case laws have been discussed [AIR 1984 Ker 73].

Case under Limitation Act 1908

Under the Limitation act, there is no period prescribed within which a petitioner for probate or letters of administration should be made after the deceased's death. It may, therefore, be presented at any time after the death of the deceased, even many years after the death. But delay in applying for probate naturally gives rise to some suspicion. If the application is made more than three years after the death, the petitioner must state the reason for the delay in his petition [AIR 1945 PC 105]. Long delay in making such application is a circumstance which may be taken into account in determining the genuineness of the will, but it is not a ground for refusing probate [(2008) 8 SCC 463, AIR 2009 SC 3247].

9.2 Components of petition for Probate [Section 276 of Indian Succession Act]

Application for probate or for letters of administration have the will annexed, along with the following components:

- The time of the testator's death

- That the writing annexed is his last will and testament

- That it was duly executed

- The amount of assets that are likely to come to the petitioner's hands

- When the application is for probate, that the petitioner is the executor named in the will

- When the application is to the district judge, that the deceased at the time of death had a fixed place of abode; and

- That the deceased at the time of death had a fixed place of abode within the jurisdiction of such delegate

The probate petition should also contain the following details:

- Details of the deceased and their legal heirs

- Details of the will, including date and circumstances of death

- Details of the property of the deceased

- Statement that the petitioners are the sole heirs as per the will and undertake to pay the duties

- Prayer to grant probate

- Affidavit of the petitioners

Details of the **deceased and legal heirs**

Details of the **will**, date and circumstances of death

Details of the **property** of the deceased

Statement that the petitioners are heirs and undertake to pay their duties

Prayer to grant probate

Affidavit of the petitioners

Figure: Illustration of the components of a probate petition or application

The petition should be made distinctly written in English or in the language in ordinary use in proceedings before the court in which the application is made.

The act lays down a rule of procedure only and not a substantive law and therefore would not make an oral will invalid. The will must be proved, and the court must be satisfied that the will has been duly executed and attested. It is enacted that with the petition for probate, the original will must be annexed excepting the will is lost or mislaid or destroyed or when the will is in the possession of outsiders. If necessary, facts regarding court fees and legal provisions are not mentioned, the application is not to be registered as sent.

Whenever possible, the exact date of the testator's death must be given. In case of disappearance of a person, on subsequent finding of his body, it must be stated that he was last seen on such and such date and the body was found on such and such date.

The writing annexed is the last will and that it was duly executed on a particular date. If the will bears a date, an affidavit of due execution referring particularly the date on which it was executed must be filed. (Section 281 of ISA 1925 Verification of petition to probate, by one witness to will). Such affidavit as far as possible should be made by one of the attesting witnesses if available. It may happen that owing to the lapse of time or other reasons that a witness cannot speak of the date with certainty. In such cases, he should endeavor to place the date of execution within a definite and limited period.

The amount and value of assets which are likely to come to the petitioner's hands and the value thereof for the purpose of probate duty. Only the properties situated in India need be mentioned. The amount and value of the property mentioned in Schedule 1, Article 11 of the Court Fees Act refer to the net value of the property. If the property is mortgaged, the value is the value of the equity of redemption.

It is obligatory for the petition to mention all the assets that are likely to come under his administration, he cannot pick and choose [ILR 22 Mad 345]. The object of this requirement is two-fold:

- assessment of duty and

- basis for testing the accuracy of the subsequent inventory and accounts to be submitted by the executor as administrator [AIR 1994 Kar 85].

The petitioner is the executor named in the will [AIR 1925 Cal 606] must prove that he was a member of firm both at the date of the will and at the time of death of the testator.

The deceased had his fixed place of abode or some property moveable or immoveable within the jurisdiction of the district judge.

Under the section [under Section 278 of ISA 1925] in a petition for probate, it is not necessary to mention the names of the next kin of testator but in practice they are required to be stated in the petition [AIR 1962 PSH 62].

When the application is made for probate to have effect throughout the whole of India, whether any application for probate or letters of administration was made to any other court and if so, what result.

The petition must be verified by the petitioner and by at least one of the attesting witnesses to the will when procurable [Section 281 of ISA 1925]. The petition for probate must be accompanied by the executor's oath. When two or more persons apply, it is not permissible to grant probate or letters of administration in fractions [(1929) 31 Bom LR 1093].

The state contemplates grant of probate or letters of administration in respect of entire estate as a general rule to be made in the circumstances indicated by the stature. In case where a part of the estate has already been administered in such a way that the part has gone to some of the heirs or legatees both in possession as well as in title, the rest of the estate is actually that of the deceased which remains to be administered by the administrator. That would constitute one of the special circumstances in which the court may make a grant of letters of administration [AIR 1988 Ker 315]

Petition for letters of administration shall be made by petitioner distinctly written (similar to probate) [Section 278 of ISA 1925].

Section 281 of ISA 1925 Verification of petition for probate by one witness to the will.

Section 282 of ISA 1925 Punishment for fake averment in petition [IPC 1860 S 193]

9.3 Some special cases

Sub section 3 [Section 276 of Indian Succession Act 1925]

The petition for probate should not be refused on the ground that there are no assets to be administered [12 CWN 129]. But in the case of a petition for letters of administration, it is the duty of the court before granting the letters of administration to see where there is any estate left to be administered [1910 14 CWN 463].

9.4 Application in forma pauperis

The order of the district judge granting or refusing probate under the section is not a decree but an order having the force of decree and of payment of the court fee, the appeal from such an order should be treated not as an appeal from a decree but as an application or petition to the high court under Schedule II article 1 of the Court Fees Act. Proceedings under ISA 1925 do not constitute a suit and the decisions on the petitioners and applications therein are not included within a definition of decree under CPC [AIR 1963 Allahabad 153]

When an executor is not in possession of the property of his testator and cannot get possession thereof and when he has not himself the means of paying the necessary fees, he may be allowed to petition, and if entitled thereto, obtain probate in forma pauperis [1893 ILR 18 Bom 237].

In case law [AIR 2005 Kant 136 in B. Manjunath vs CG Srinivas] it held that in a proceeding or application filed for grant of probate or letters of administration, since no right was asserted or claimed by an applicant and the applicant only sought recognition of the court to perform duty, the application filed for issue of probate did not fall within Article 137 of the Limitation Act.

AIR 2008 SC 2058/ AIR 1991 Mad 214 - Para 51

Kunvarjeet Singh v Kirandeep Kaur / S Krishnaswami v E Ramiah

In para 17 of the said judgement it was noted as follows: [AIR p222]

In a proceeding, or in other words, in an application filed for grant of probate or letters of administration, no right is asserted or claimed by the applicant. The applicant only seeks recognition of the court to perform a duty. Probate or letters of administration issued by a competent court is conclusive proof of the legal character throughout the world. An assessment of the relevant provisions of the Indian Succession Act, 1925 does not convey a meaning that by the proceedings filed for grant of probate or letters of administration, no rights of the applicant are settled or secured in the legal sense. The author of the testament has cast the duty with regard to the administration of his estate, and the applicant for probate or letters of administration only seeks the permission of the court to perform that duty. There is only a seeking of recognition from the court to perform the duty. That duty is only moral and it is not legal. There is no law which compels the applicant to file the proceedings for probate or letters of administration. With a view to discharge the moral duty, the applicant seeks recognition from the court to perform the duty. It will be legitimate to conclude that the proceedings filed for grant of probate or letters of administration is not an action in law. Hence, it is very difficult to and it will not be in order to construe the proceedings for grant of probate or letters of administration as applications coming within the meaning of an "application" under Article 137 of the Limitation Act, 1963.

9.5 Source from which costs are to be provided

Under Section 293 of ISA 1925, in case of an application for probate, seven clear days must be allowed to pass after the death of the testator before an application can be entertained, and 14 days must pass after the death of the testator or intestate for an application for letters of administration.

The decision of the revenue court touching the will does not operate as res-judicata in the probate proceeding in which the sole question involved is as to the proof of the will.

9.6 A sample probate application

A sample petition for probate is as follows:

IN THE COURT OF ____

Probate case No. __ of __ <year>

In the matter of

Mr __ <petitioner name>

Resident of ___ (Petitioner)

versus

State (Respondents)

Probate petition under section 276 of the Indian Succession Act on behalf of the petitioners for grant of probate in respect of the will dated ___ executed by ___ son of ___ resident of ___ in favour of the petitioners namely __.

MOST RESPECTFULLY SHOWETH:

1. That ___, son of ___, resident of ___, hereafter known as the deceased, who was a Hindu governed by the Hindu Succession Act, died on ___ at ___, which was his fixed place of residence. A copy of the death certificate issued by the sub-registrar of births and deaths is annexed herewith as Annexure A.

2. That at the time of death, the deceased was about __ years of age. During his life time, the deceased duly executed a will dated __ in respect of moveable and immoveable property bearing ___.

3. That at the time of death, the deceased left behind the following legal heirs:

i) name, address, age, relationship

ii) name, address, age, relationship

iii) name, address, age, relationship

4. That prior to his death, the deceased executed the will dated ___ in favour of ___ and ___

5. That the deceased was competent to execute the will dated __ , being the owner of the property at ___ having the following details:

6. That it is submitted that through the said will, the deceased bequeathed the said property in the following manner:

i)

ii)

iii)

7. That the petitioners after the death of ___ became the sole executors/legal heirs of the deceased testator as per the will in respect of the property mentioned herein above.

8. That late ____ was residing in ___ , died in ___ on the date ___ . Further the property left behind by the deceased was situated in ___ , which is within the jurisdiction of this honourable court.

9. That the will dated __ is annexed to the affidavit of ___, who is one of the attesting witnesses.

10. That the value of the assets of said deceased beyond the limit of the State of __ does not exceed Rs. ___ .

11. That to the best of the petitioner's knowledge, no application has been made to any High Court or other District Court for probate of the said will.

12. That the petitioner undertakes to pay the duty payable for the grant of probate.

PRAYER

The petitioner therefore most respectfully prays that in the facts and circumstances of the case the probate in respect of the will dated ___ executed by late ___ be granted in favour of the petitioners, in the interest of justice.

For such other order/relief/direction as this honourable court may deem just and proper be also passed in favour of the petitioners.

AFFIDAVIT

I, ___, son of ___, aged___, resident of ___, do hereby solemnly affirm and declare as under:

1. That I am the petitioner no. 1 and am well conversant with the facts of the case.

2. That the facts stated in the accompanying petition have been drafted by our counsel under my instructions which are all true and correct.

(Signed)

At:

Dated:

9.7 Court procedure for a probate application

Note: The exact procedure may vary in different Indian states. But generally, the steps are as follows:

- The petitioners submit the probate application at an appropriate court in the prescribed format, along with the accompanying documents such as death certificate, affidavits and court fees

- Court receives the application and verifies the details

- Court directs to publish in leading newspapers a notice inviting the members of the public and next of kin of the deceased to file any objections. It also directs to send notification letters to the next of kin at their addresses mentioned in the probate application, informing them of the application of probate.

- If after a period of time, there is no objection, the court issues the probate and letters of administration, upon payment of the court fees (which depend on the value of the assets).

- If there is an objection from one or more of the parties, the issuance of probate is delayed. The normal court procedure takes place, with presentation of evidence, arguments and cross examination from the parties. After examining the evidence and arguments, the court issues its judgment regarding the grant of probate and letters of administration.

9.8 Common Grounds for Rejection or Objection of Probate

Probate may be denied if the will appears forged, lacks attestation, is revoked by a later will, or is challenged due to lack of testamentary capacity or coercion.

9.9 Alternative Remedies if Probate Is Denied

If probate is denied, parties may try the following remedial actions:

- Appeal the decision in higher courts
- File for letters of administration (if no valid will exists)
- Pursue a civil suit for declaratory rights over the property

9.10 Conclusion

Filing for probate is essential, yet complications can arise if the will itself is contested on grounds of fraud or coercion. The following chapter will address these significant challenges, offering insights into how courts address wills that may have been compromised by fraud, coercion, or undue influence.

Chapter 10: Common Litigation: Will Disputes and Resolution

While a well-drafted will can bring clarity and peace to families, will disputes are unfortunately common in India. Such litigation can be time-consuming, expensive, and emotionally draining. Understanding the common grounds for will disputes, how such cases proceed in court, and the best methods of resolution can help both testators and beneficiaries avoid pitfalls and resolve conflicts effectively.

10.1 Why Are Wills Disputed?

Will disputes typically arise due to the following factors:

- Perceived unfairness in the distribution of assets.

- Doubts about the will's authenticity (forgery, suspicious circumstances).

- Allegations of undue influence or coercion over the testator.

- Challenges to the testator's mental capacity at the time of making the will.

- Omissions or ambiguities in the will's wording.

- Family dynamics—rivalries, second marriages, step-children, and blended families.

- Multiple wills or codicils leading to confusion about the testator's final wishes.

10.2 Grounds for Contesting a Will in India

Common legal grounds for contesting a will include the following:

- Lack of Testamentary Capacity: The challenger claims the testator did not have a sound mind or understanding when making the will. Courts look for medical evidence, witness testimony, and circumstantial proof.

- Undue Influence, Fraud, or Coercion: If someone in a position of power manipulates the testator or if the will is procured by fraud or threat, it can be set aside.

- Forgery or Fraud: Allegations that the signature or the entire document is forged, or that pages have been replaced or manipulated.

- Improper Execution or Attestation: A will not signed by the testator, or not properly attested by two witnesses as required by law, can be invalid.

- Revocation by a Later Will or Codicil: If a new will or codicil is discovered, it can revoke an earlier will wholly or partially.

- Ambiguity or Uncertainty: Vague language, contradictory clauses, or failure to specify assets or beneficiaries can render all or part of a will invalid.

- Suspicious Circumstances: Where there are circumstances that arouse suspicion—such as the main beneficiary preparing the will, sudden changes shortly before death, or exclusion of natural heirs—the court will scrutinize the will more closely.

10.3 Who Can Contest a Will?

The persons who can contest a will include the following:

- Legal heirs (children, spouse, parents, etc.) who would benefit if the will is set aside.

- Other beneficiaries named or omitted in the will.

- Any person with an interest in the estate (including creditors in rare cases).

10.4 Procedure for Disputing a Will

The procedure includes the following steps:

a) Filing a Caveat

If someone intends to oppose the grant of probate or letters of administration, they can file a caveat in the relevant court, preventing the issuance of probate without notice to them.

b) Probate Proceedings

If the will's validity is challenged, the probate process becomes contentious. The burden of proof lies on the propounder (the person seeking probate) to establish due execution and genuineness. The challenger must provide evidence of the alleged defects.

c) Evidence and Trial

Courts examine the will, hear witnesses (including attesting witnesses, doctors, and handwriting experts if needed), and assess the overall circumstances.

d) Judgment and Appeal

After considering all evidence, the court may grant or deny probate. An appeal can be made to a higher court if either party is dissatisfied.

10.5 Key Court Principles in Will Dispute Cases

Some of the key court principles include:

- Onus of Proof: The person propounding the will must prove its validity, especially where suspicious circumstances exist.

- Testator's Intention: The court's primary aim is to determine and give effect to the testator's true intention.

- Presumption of Regularity: If a will appears regular and is attested properly, courts tend to uphold it unless strong evidence to the contrary is shown.

- Suspicious Circumstances: Where suspicion arises, courts require greater scrutiny and evidence to dispel doubts.

Case example:

In Jaswant Kaur v. Amrit Kaur (1977), the Supreme Court held that where a will was shrouded in suspicious circumstances, the burden is on the propounder to dispel suspicion. If the court's conscience is not satisfied, probate may be denied.

10.6 Alternative Dispute Resolution (ADR) in Will Disputes

With growing court backlogs and the emotional toll of family litigation, ADR methods such as mediation and family settlement agreements are increasingly encouraged.

Some of these include:

- Mediation: Many family will disputes are resolved with the help of a neutral mediator, often resulting in settlements that preserve relationships.

- Family Settlements: Indian law recognizes family settlements, even informal ones, provided all parties are adults and agree voluntarily. Such settlements can override the will if all beneficiaries consent.

Tip: Whenever possible, attempt to resolve disputes outside court to save time, money, and relationships.

10.7 Preventive Measures to Avoid Will Disputes

Preventative measures a person can take to avoid will disputes among their successors include the following:

- Clear and unambiguous drafting of the will.

- Explicit reasoning for exclusion of natural heirs (if any).

- Medical certificate of soundness at the time of execution, especially for elderly or ill testators.

- Use of independent witnesses and professional drafting services.

- Registration of the will (optional, but can help as evidence).

- Communication with heirs about the testator's wishes (where appropriate).

10.8 Checklist: Steps for Beneficiaries Facing a Will Dispute

Beneficiaries of a will can follow the following checklist of steps:

- Consult a lawyer experienced in succession law.

- Gather documents: The will, medical records, previous wills, property papers, correspondence.

- File a caveat if you suspect probate may be granted without your knowledge.

- Consider mediation or negotiation before or alongside court proceedings.

- Prepare for evidence: Line up witnesses and obtain expert reports if needed.

10.9 Conclusion

Will disputes are unfortunately a reality in India's complex social and legal environment. But with proper drafting, awareness of common pitfalls, and openness to settlement, many disputes can be avoided or resolved amicably. A legally sound and well-communicated will remains the best safeguard against future litigation.

Chapter 11: Wills Obtained by Fraud, Coercion and Importunity

In this chapter, we discuss some important special cases that can result in wills becoming invalidated: that of fraud, coercion, and importunity.

11.1 Section 61 of Indian Succession Act 1925

A will or any part of a will, the making of which has been caused by fraud or coercion or by such importunity as takes away the free agency of the testator, is void.

11.2 Persons capable of making wills [Section 59 of Indian Succession Act 1925]

Every person of sound mind and not being a minor may dispose of his property by will. Therefore, generally speaking, all persons who have sufficient discretion and free will are capable of disposing of their property by will.

As to the testator's capacity, he must, in the language of law, have a sound disposing mind and memory. In other words, he ought to be capable of making his will with an understanding of the nature of the business in which he is engaged, a recollection of the property he means to dispose of, of the persons who are the objects of his bounty, and the manner in which it is to be distributed between them. It is sufficient if he has such a mind and memory as will enable him to understand the elements of which it is composed and the disposition of the property in simple forms. [(1873) LR3 PSD64]

It must be shown that the testator was of a sound disposing mind at the time when the will or codicil was made. The law requires that there should be a sound disposing mind at the time when the instructions for the will are given and the will is executed.

Sound testamentary capacity means that these conditions must exist at one and the same time:

- The testator must understand that he is giving his property one or more objects of his regard

- He must understand and recollect the extent of this property

- He must also understand the nature and extent of claims upon him, both of those he is including in his will and those whom he is excluding from the will.

The testator must realize that he is seizing a will in his mind and the will must accompany his physical act of execution [Williams, Law of Wills, 3rd Edition, p-16].

11.3 Burden of proving a will

Where a plea of undue influence is set up, Section 103 of the Evidence Act 1872 places the burden of substantiating such a plea on the party which sets it up [AIR 1974 SC 1999].

11.4 Burden of proving the testamentary capacity of the testator

The burden always lies with the party propounding the will to satisfy the conscience of the court that the testator, at the time of executing the will, was of sound and disposing state of mind [AIR 1968, SC 947]. But in the absence of any evidence as to the state of the testator's mind, proof that he had executed a will rational in character in the presence of witnesses must lead to a presumption that he was of sound mind and understood what it was about. The presumption was held as justified under the express provision of Section 90 of the Evidence Act 1972 and further fortified under Section 114 where a will more than 30 years old was produced [AIR 1947 PC 15].

Generally speaking, every person is presumed to be sane until he is proved to be insane. Whenever, therefore, a will is produced which on the face of it is validly executed, the court will presume that the testator was sane [AIR 1956 Bom 404]. The presumption of sanity is a mixed presumption of law and fact. In probate suits, the ultimate burden of proving testamentary capacity rests on the party propounding the will. If any party alleges that the testator was insane, then it will lie on the party propounding the will to prove affirmatively that the testator was of sound mind at the date of the execution of the will and that he knew and understood and approved of its contents [(1905) 7 Bom LR 175].

A testator may disinherit his children to gratify his spite or benefit charity to gratify his pride, but the court must nevertheless uphold the will. Testamentary capacity thus calls for particular mental characteristics. A man may have the mental capacity to marry and yet, on his wedding day, be incapable of making a will [Williams and Mortimer Adms and Probate 16th Edition].

In Pallavi vs Ramachandran [2000 6 SCC 151]: The testator had executed two wills on the same day, one setting up a trust for performance of religious charity and another, making a bequest in respect of his personal properties. The execution of one was admitted by the party and the mutual capacity admitting the other will was disputed. The Supreme Court rejected the stand as the parties cannot blow hot and cold. The admission of valid extension regarding the mutual capacity of one meant the valid testamentary capacity of the other will also.

As to the testator's capacity, he must, in the language of law, have a sound and disposing mind and memory. In other words, he ought to be capable of making his will with an understanding of the nature of the business in which he is engaged, a recollection of the property he means to dispose of, of the persons who are the objects of his bounty, and the manner in which it is to be distributed between them. It is sufficient, if he has such a mind and memory as will enable him to understand the elements of which it is composed and the disposition of his property in simple forms [(1870) LR5QB549567]

If a will is registered, that is a circumstance which many, having regard to the circumstances, prove its genuineness. [AIR 1962 SC 567, AIR 1968 SC 947]

11.5 Grounds for lacking testamentary capacity

There are two grounds on which a person may be held to lack testamentary capacity:

- That his mind has never developed sufficiently

- That his mind is impaired, temporarily or permanently

There are a number of causes of impairment of mind such as physical injury, physical illness, addiction to drink or drugs, sevility or mental illness.

When a will's validity is challenged due to mental incapacity, courts may order medical records or expert testimony. Psychiatric assessments can be pivotal in proving or disproving free will.

11.6 Will obtained by Fraud

A will which is the result of one or the other kind of fraud, is null and void [Boyce v Rosenbrough, 6 HLC2].

A fraud is an act of deliberate deception with the design of securing something by taking unfair advantage of another. It is the deception in order to gain by another's loss. It is a cheating intended to get an advantage [SP Chengalvanya v Jagannath AIR 1994 SC 853].

Fraud arises out of a deliberate active role of representation about a fact which he knows to be untrue, yet he succeeds in misleading the representee by making him believe it to be true. The representation to become fraudulent must be of fact made with the knowledge that it was false [Shristi v Shaw Bros. AIR 1992 SC 1555].

Fraud is a false misrepresentation by one who is aware that it was untrue with an intention to mislead the other who may act upon it to his prejudice and to the advantage of the representator [State of Maharashtra v Buddhikota AIR 1989 SC 2292].

Being infinite, the court does not define the term "fraud". It has been described as an act of trickery or deceit. Some definitions from dictionaries are as follows:

- Webster's third New International Dictionary - Fraud in equity has been defined as an act or omission to act or concealment by which one person obtains an advantage against conscience over another or which equity or public policy forbids as being prejudicial to another.

- Black's law dictionary – fraud is defined as an intentional perversion of truth for the purpose of inducing another in reliance upon it to part with some valuable thing belonging to him or surrender a legal right; a false representation of a matter of fact whether by words or conduct, by false or misleading allegations, or by concealment of that which should have been disclosed, which deceives and is intended to deceive another so that he shall act upon it to his legal injury.

- Halisbury's Laws of England – a representation is deemed to have been false and therefore a misrepresentation, if it was at the material date false in substance and in fact.

Although it is not exactly correct to say that fraud must be proved with strictures of a criminal charge, there is no doubt that a very high degree of proof is needed to establish it [William and Mortimer 16th Ed p 173].

Fraud, in all cases, implies a willful act on the part of anyone whereby, another is sought to be deprived by illegal or inequitable means, of something which he is entitled to [Green v Nixon (1857) 23 Bear 530].

If the legatee induced the testator to believe what was not true, that his wife was of bad character and had left his house, it was held that the will was procured by misrepresentation and fraud [AIR 1929 Oudh 262].

Fraud has been defined in Section 17 of the Contract Act which is but an explanation.

Fraud is either actual or constructive. Actual fraud is sub divided into two parts:

- misrepresentation and

- concealment.

Misrepresentation (called suggestio falsi) must be of a material fact and must have been relied or acted upon by the person deceived.

Concealment (called suppresio veri) is the suppression or withholding of some material fact, being some fact which one party was under the legal duty to the other to disclose [Turner v Green (1895) 2 CH 205, AIR 1953 SC 163, AIR 1956 MB 246, 249].

Effect of fraud: the effect of fraud on any processing or transaction is that it becomes a nullity. Even the most solemn proceedings stand vitiated if they are actuated by fraud. Such being the nature and consequence o it, the law requires not only strict pleading of it but strict proof as well.

11.7 Will obtained by Coercion

Compulsion by physical force or threat of physical force, conduct that constitutes the improper use of economic power to compel another to submit to the wishes of one who wields it [Black's Law Dictionary].

Coercion takes an infinite number of forms, but it may properly be thus defined: the moment that the person who influences the other does so by the threat of taking away from that other something that he then possesses, or by preventing him from obtaining an advantage he would otherwise have obtained, then it becomes coercion and ceases to be persuasion or consideration [Ellis v Barker (1871) 40 LJ Ch 603/607].

Coercion is defined by Section 15 of the Contract Act 1872 as "the committing or threatening to commit any act forbidden by law (IPC) or the unlawful deterring or threatening to detain any property to the prejudice of any person whatever with the intention of causing any person to enter into an agreement." It is the first portion of the definition which would properly apply. To constitute undue influence in the eyes of the law, there must be coercion.

Whatever destroys the free agency of the testator constitutes coercion. If actual force was used to compel the testator to make the will and all the formalities are complied with, yet the will is void [1 Cox 355].

Examples of coercion are as follows:

- Threat to commit suicide is coercion [AIR 1969 Cal 293].

- Coercion in Section 72 of the Contract Act must be understood in the ordinary sense. In includes every kind of compulsion even if it does not measure up to the definition under Section 15 of the Contract Act [AIR 1969 MYS 230]

- If actual force was used to compel the testator to make the will and all the formalities are completed with, yet the will is void [1 Cox 355]: So also if the testator is laboring under some fear at the time of bequeathing. But it is not every fear or vain fear that will have the effect of annulling the will, but just the fear that the law can take cognizance of, such as the fear or death, or of bodily hurt, or imprisonment.

- A threatens to shoot B, or to burn his house, or to cause him to be arrested on a criminal charge, unless he makes a bequest in favor of C. B in consequence makes a bequest in favor of C. The bequest is void, the making of it having been caused by coercion [AIR 1922 Cal 260].

- The conduct of a person in vigorous health towards one feeble in body, even though not of unsound mind, may be such as to excite a terror and make execute his will, an instrument which if had been free from such influence, he would not have executed [(1857) 6 HLC 2].

- In order to come to the conclusion that a will has been obtained by coercion, it is not necessary to establish that actual violence has been used or threatened [AIR 1922 Cal 260 / (2013) 2 Mah LJ 161].

11.8 Will obtained by importunity and undue influence

Undue influence is the improper use of power or trust in a way that deprives a person of free will and substitutes another's objective [Black's Law Dictionary: 8th Edition].

Undue influence includes any influence in which the exercise of free and deliberate judgement is excluded. Undue influence is presumed until the contrary is proved when the relation of the parties is such that one is entitled to the confidential advice of the other, as in the case of solicitor and client, of a trustee and trust and of a parent contracting with a child who has first come of age. In other cases of confidential relationship, the party seeking to avoid a contract must prove undue influence [Sutton and Shannon on Contracts 6th Edition].

Every influence cannot be characterized as undue. A done can appeal and persuade the donor to make a gift to him. Such appeals and persuasions cannot be characterized as undue influence, provided the donor retains the mental capacity [Takri Devi v Rama AIR 1984 HP 11, 15, Subhas v Ganga Prasad AIR 1967 SC 878, Afsar v Solamn AIR 1976 SC 163].

When the will of the testator is coerced into doing that which he or she does not intend to do, it is undue influence [Boudams v Richardson (1906) AC 169].

Undue influence means the presence of whatever character if so exercised as to overpower the volition without convincing the judgment of the testator though no force is either used or threatened. There must be positive proof of coercion, overpowering the volition of the testator.

Undue influence as defined in Section 16 of the Contract Act 1872, is that relation which subsists between the parties by which one of the parties is in a position to dominate the will of the other and uses that position to obtain an unfair advantage over that other [AIR 1996 Ker 64, AIR 1956 MB 246, AIR 1960 Cal 551, AIR 1979 SC 1431, Barry and Butler – AIR 1976 Cal 377, AIR 1955 SC 363, AIR 1968 SC 964].

Proof of motive and opportunity for the exercise of such influences is required, but the existence of such, coupled with the fact that the person who has such motive and opportunity has benefitted by the will to the exclusion of others, is not sufficient to prove undue influence. [Williams, Law of Wills, 3rd Edition, p 24].

A son who lived with his father (testator), even if he was found to have used persuasion and appeals to affection and evoked sentiment of great ends, could not be said to have used undue influence [AIR 1996 Ker 64].

Undue influence is 'coercion' only if it takes away the free agency of the testator. Whatever takes away the free agency of the testator, constitutes coercion [11 CWN 824].

The mere fact that in making his will he was influenced by immoral [(1906) AC 169] or irreligious [(1893) 1 Ch 736] consideration does not amount to such undue influence, so long as the disposition contained in the will really express his wishes.

Importunity in its correct legal acceptation must be in such a degree as to take away from the testator free agency - it must be of such importunity as he is too weak to resist, such as will render the act no longer the act of the deceased; nor the free act of a capable testator, in order to invalidate an instrument.

11.9 Execution of a will during lucid intervals

When there was a medical report of a clinical psychologist that the testator was suffering from chronic schizophrenia, the history of the previous psychiatric treatment with the following symptoms: poor rapport, irrelevant talk, inappropriate effect, paranoid delusions, auditory hallucinations, no organic features, no insight and no judgment, a circumstance that he had obtained a cheque through court cannot itself provide the basis that the will could also have been executed during a lucid interval, is a matter to be pleaded and proved. It is not sufficient to prove that the testator had lucid intervals. Proof that he executed the will during a lucid interval is necessary. In the absence of such proofs, coupled with the fact that the propounder's deceased husband had earlier applied for appointment of himself as a guardian for the property o the testator and her own admission that she had also filed a similar application but later had it dismissed as withdrawn were taken as establishing that the will could not be taken to be of a person with sound mind [Trese Xavier v Mary Simon No 240 of 2003, decided on 01.09.2014].

Unsoundness of mind may be occasioned by physical infirmity or advancing years as distinguished from mental derangement and the resulting defeat of intelligence may be the cause of incapacity, but the intelligence must be reduced to such an extent that the proposed testator does not appreciate the testamentary act in all its bearings. Old age or the near approach of death at any age, lend strength to the suggestion that the testator had proper knowledge of the contents of the will [Williams, Law of Wills pp. 20-21].

11.10 Inofficious statements

In case of *inofficious* statements, i.e. when a testator gives away his property to strangers forgetting his natural duty to his children, there is no presumption of insanity, but it may throw some light upon the questions of the testator's capacity [Halisbury's Laws of England]. The court always looks upon such a will with grave suspicion, especially when such a will is produced after a lapse of many years [Musammal v Alma 64 IA 92].

The propounder of the will has to show that the will was signed by the testator, that he was at the relevant time in a sound disposing state of mind, that he understood the nature and the effect of the dispositions, that he had signed in the presence of two witnesses who attested it in his presence and in the presence of each other. Once these elements are established, the onus which rests on the propounder is discharged [Surendra Pal v Dr. Sarswati AIR 1974 SC 1999].

11.11 Conclusion

Understanding the gravity of invalid wills, we must ensure that the execution of wills is always compliant with legal standards. The next chapter provides critical guidelines on the execution of unprivileged wills, outlining clear procedural steps to ensure the validity and enforceability of wills under Indian law.

Chapter 12: Execution of Unprivileged Wills

In this chapter, we discuss important points of law in proving a will to be genuine: such as the nature of suspicious circumstances and valid attestation.

12.1 Rules for the execution of wills

Execution of the will is done according to the following rules:

- The testator shall sign or shall affix his marks to the will

- The signature or mark should be so placed that it shall appear that it was intended thereby to give effect to the writing as a will

- The will shall be attested by two or more persons (witnesses) each of whom seen the testator sign to the will and each of the witnesses shall sign the will in front of the testator

- It must be dated. If the will is not dated, proof of the day on which the will was executed to be given when petition of probate is filed (AIR 2013 Delhi 220)

12.2 Onus which rests on the testator

The propounder has to show that the will was signed by the testator, that he was at the relevant time in a sound disposing state of mind, that he understood the nature and effect of the dispositions, that he put his signature to the testament of his own free will and that he has signed it in the presence of two witnesses who attested it in his presence and in the presence of each other [AIR 1974 SC 1999].

It is for the propounder of the will to prove the will of execution and attestation and in the absence of suspicious circumstances surrounding the execution of the will, proof of testamentary capacity and signature of the testator as required by law is sufficient to discharge the onus which is placed upon the propounder of the will [AIR 1972 SC 2492].

12.3 Position where there are 'suspicious circumstances'

Where there are suspicious circumstances, the propounder of the will has to explain them away to the satisfaction of the court. The suspicious circumstances may be as to the genuineness of the signature of the testator, the condition of the testator's mind, the dispositions made in the will being unnatural, improbable or unfair in the light of relevant circumstances, or there may be other indications in the will to show that the testator's mind was not free. But where there are suspicious circumstances the onus will be on the propounder to explain them to the satisfaction of the court before the will could be accepted as genuine; and where the caveator alleges undue influence, fraud and coercion the onus is on him to prove the same [AIR 1972 SC 2492 /AIR 1974 SC 1999]

Suspicious circumstances (AIR 1972 Patna 146)

The fact that Mukhlal, the testator in this instant case was aged about 80 years at the time of the execution of the will and that his signature on the will was shaky due to old age or due to certain disease from which he suffered would not by themselves be enough to hold that these are suspicious circumstances.

The appellant had taken active interest in the execution of the will, the propounder was merely present at the time of the execution of the will

Scribe of the will does not support the case at all - the witness was hostile to the appellant and deliberately telling lies.

Even in AIR 1959 SC 443 their lordships at page 459 pointed out what circumstances would be regarded as suspicious circumstances cannot be precisely defined or exhaustively enumerated.

12.4 Observations by honorable judges in some cases

Case AIR 1959 SC 443 F/B Three judges

The party propounding a will or otherwise making a claim under a will is no doubt seeking to prove a document and, in deciding how it is to be proved, reference must inevitably be made to the statutory provisions which govern the proof of documents.

Section 67 and 68 of the Evidence Act are relevant for the purpose. Under section 67 of the Evidence Act, if a document is alleged to be signed by any person, the signature of the said person must be proved to be in his own handwriting and for proving such handwriting section 45 and 47 of the Act, the opinions or experts and of persons acquainted with handwriting of the person concerned are made relevant.

Section 68 of the Evidence Act deals with proof of execution of the documents required by law to be attested and it provides that such document shall not be used as evidence unless one attesting witness at least has been called for the purpose of proving its execution. Similarly, Sections 59 and 63 of the ISA 1925 are also relevant.

Thus the question as to whether will set up by the propounder is proved to be the last will of the testator has to be decided in the light of these provisions. It would prima facie be true to tell that the will has to be proved like any other document except as to the special requirement of attestation prescribed in Section 63 of ISA 1925. As in the case of proof of other documents so in the case of proof of wills it would be idle to expect proof with mathematical certainty. The test to be applied would be the usual test of the satisfaction of the prudent mind in such matters.

12.5 Vagueness of the will

If the contents of the will are found to be vague despite the genuineness thereof, the grant of probate in favor of the applicant may be declined [AIR 2006 SC 1999].

It is not for probate court to exercise its jurisdiction to make an interpretation of the will [2009 IKLJ 865].

The jurisdiction does not extend beyond the truth of execution as regards the mental capacity of the executant and the validity of the attestation.

12.6 Can Video or Audio Recordings Be Used to Prove a Will?

Though not a substitute for written wills, video recordings can serve as supporting evidence of voluntariness and capacity. However, they must comply with evidentiary rules and may not override statutory formalities.

12.7 Role of the Registrar as Witness or Verifier

When registering a will, the Sub-Registrar ensures voluntary execution but does not verify content. While not mandatory, registration strengthens authenticity and reduces disputes.

12.8 Signature of the testator

- The will shall be signed by the testator or shall have his mark affixed to it.

- It can be signed by some other person but in the testator's presence but also by his direction.

- It must be dated. If the will is not dated, proof of the day may be given when the petition for probate is filed.

Section 63(a) of the ISA 1925 provides that the testator can sign or affix his mark. Even if the testator is capable of writing but on account of weakness he is unable to put his signature, he can execute a will by affixing a mark and in doing so his hand may be guided by another person [AIR 1962 Pat 481]. Such a thumb impression is held to be valid [AIR 1991 Cal 166]. In Leela Karwal v JD Karwal [AIR 1986 All 220] it was held that the requirement of signing the will by the testator is for the purpose of authenticating the contents of the writing containing his declaration about the disposition of his property after his death. It is, therefore, apparent that the testator has to put his signature or mark as contemplated by Section 63(3) of the ISA 1925 Act only after the contents of the writing containing the declaration has been scribed, for it is not possible to authenticate a declaration before such a declaration has been actually scribed and has come into existence.

When some pages of the will are not signed, it is not a suspicious circumstance as only one signature on the last page is sufficient [AIR 1996 Mad 442].

If the person signs for the testator, besides himself there must be two other persons as attesting witnesses [(1881) ILR 6 Cal 483].

12.9 Place of signature of the testator

The signature of mark of the testator may be placed anywhere either at the commencement or at the end, but it must be so placed that it shall appear that it is intended to give effect to the instrument as a will. In the case of absence of signature of the testator on the appendix, it has been held by the Supreme Court that in such a situation, the will was therefore not complete [AIR 2008 SC 2195].

12.10 Suspicious signature

In Zaruna R Irani v Shapar Jawanmandi apart from delayed publication, the signature of the testator had been seen through a tracer, which was found to be the most or gravest suspicious circumstance [(2004) 6 Bom CR 142]. The deviation of the signature from the usual mode of the signature of the testator was found to be suspicious [(2005) 3 CHN 259].

Natural texture and clarity of the signature of the testatrix differing from page to page was taken to be a suspicious document [(2009) 7 MLJ 135]. If the signature is attacked as forgery, the propounder is bound to adduce proof of the signature. It was however held by the Madras High Court in a judgement [(2010) (1) AIHLR 268] that the person who alleges forgery must establish the same.

Firm signature, although with some overwriting: Where the handwriting of the testator is clear and firm though there was some overwriting found almost all of the times, the court said that it could not be attributed to any other prescription but to the age of the testator and definitely not against the genuineness of the will [(2009) 5 MLJ 245].

12.11 Court's power to compare signatures

Court has the power to compare the signature in the will of the testator with his other admitted signatures, but it cannot itself dispense with the requirements of proof as per the section and under article Section 68 of the Evidence Act.

12.12 Form of attestation

No particular form of attestation is necessary clause [(1960) 10 Raj 1259]. The will shall be attested by two or more witnesses. It is a mandate of law and must be proved as such [2014 (1) OLR 788].

- Each witness must have seen the testator sign or affix his mark

- Each witness must have seen some other person sign the will in the presence of and by the direction of the testator.

- If the will is already signed, each witness must have received from the testator a personal acknowledgement of his signature or mark or of the signature of such person signing for him.

It is not, however, necessary, that both the witnesses should be present at one and the same time [19 CWN 1297]. In so far as the attesting witnesses are concerned, the only statutory requisite is that they should have the necessary *animus testatandi* or intention to attest the document. If one of the attestors speaks of the signature of the testator, then it is enough and no further proof is necessary to satisfy whether the signature as acknowledged has been affixed [AIR 1977 SC 63].

The testator may sign in the presence of one witness and acknowledge his signature before another witness. The words 'in his presence' means not only the physical presence of the testator but the mental presence i.e. the deceased must be in his senses [(1948) All ER 700].

12.13 Evidence of due execution and attestation

A party who puts forward a document as being the true last will of the deceased must establish that the testator knew and approved of the contents at the time when he executed it. Testator's knowledge and approval of the contents of the will are part of the burden of proof assumed by everyone who propounds a testamentary document. Under normal circumstances, this burden is discharged by proof of testamentary capacity and due extension, from which knowledge and approval of the contents can be assumed. But there may be circumstances where knowledge and approval have to be affirmatively proved. Affirmative evidence of knowledge and approval may be required when a will is alleged to have been signed by another person for the deceased and at his direction [Williams and Mortimer 16th edition, pp 158-159].

The mode of proving a will does not ordinarily differ from any other document, except as to the special requirement of attestation prescribed by Section 63 of the ISA 1925 Act. Proof in either case cannot be mathematically precise and certain, and hence the test should be one of satisfaction of a prudent mind in such matters [AIR 1971 SC 2236].

12.14 Standard of proof

The standard of proof to establish a will required by the Act is that of the prudent man and not an absolute or conclusive one [AIR 1959 SC443]. A will is one of the most solemn documents known to law. But if a dead man entrusts to the living the carrying out of his wishes and as it is impossible that he can be called either to deny his signature or to explain the circumstances in which it was made, it is essential that trustworthy and effective evidence should be given to establish the will. In case of dispute or doubt the best evidence possible should be furnished [AIR 1922 PC 366].

In ordinary cases, execution of a will by a competent testator raises the presumption that he knew and approved the contents of the will [(1898) ILR 2521 Cal 279] (Rashmohini v Woomesh Chuder). Unless it can be established that a will was executed by fraud or not in fit and disposing mind, it cannot be thrown away merely on suspicion [1957 All LJ 667] (Jamuna v Har Dasi). The test to be applied regarding the proof of the will, will be the usual test of the satisfaction of the court as a prudent person in such matters. But it shall be the duty of the propounder to remove all suspicions about the execution or about the disposing state of mind of the testator. If he fails to do so, the court shall be reluctant to treat the document as the last will of the testator [Ramrani v Madanlal AIR 1973 Raj 295].

As regards proof of the signature of the testator, the best evidence available, viz. the evidence of attesting witnesses, should be given and any evidence of a general nature to the effect that the signature appears to be genuine is of little worth [AIR 1922 Cal 260]. But the mere fact that the attesting witnesses have repudiated their signature does not invalidate the will, if it can be proved by evidence of a reliable character [Brahmadut v Chandan 20 Cal CWN 192].

12.15 Burden of proof

Nature and standard of evidence required

There is a long line of decisions on the nature and standard of evidence required to prove a will. All those decisions were reviewed in H Venkatachala Iyenger v BN Thimmajamna [AIR 1959 SC443] and the Supreme Court laid down six propositions of law. In any case the burden of proof does not vary with the riches and social prestige of the testator. Normally, a genuine will of a propertied man, well positioned in a society does not suffer from the loopholes and infirmities which may understandably beset a humbler testamentary instrument [Jaswant Kaur v Arun Kaur AIR 1977 SC 74].

Where there are suspicious circumstances the onus is on the propounder to explain them to the satisfaction of the court before the court accepts the will as genuine [Sashi Kr v Subodh Kr AIR 1964 SC 529]. In the case of a will, it would be idle to expect proof with mathematical certainty [Shri Ram v Kasturi AIR 1984 All 66] relied on [AIR 1959 SC 443, AIR 1964 SC 529, AIR 1965 SC 354].

Rule in Barry v Butlin (1838) 2 MOO PCC 480

If a party writes or prepares a will under which he takes a benefit, that is a circumstance which ought generally to excite the suspicion of the court and calls upon it to be vigilant and zealous in examining the evidence in support of the instrument in favor of which it ought not to pronounce unless the suspicion is removed and it is judicially satisfied that the paper does express the true will of the deceased [AIR 1962 SC 567].

12.16 Revocation of unprivileged will or codicil

Revocation of will is divided into two parts by its section.

- By an operation of law (e.g. by marriage) as provided in Section 69 of ISA 1925, and

- By acts of parties (e.g. by another will or codicil, or by some other writing, or by burning, tearing or otherwise destroying). The modes of revocation as prescribed in this section are exhaustive [AIR 1922 Cal 182].

The revocation of previous wills or codicils must be expressly and definitely made and it is not sufficient to say that this will is the last will as that statement does not amount to a revocation of a former will. The intention to revoke a will should be expressly declared [Section 70 of ISA 1925].

A will can be either changed or revoked. But alteration or revocation has to take place before the death of the testator. The latter must sign any amendment, or codicil, in the presence of witnesses – exactly as when the original was executed.

As a rule, an express revoking clause will operate to revoke all the contents of prior wills or codicils. Thus, a will executing a special power of appointment is revoked in tote by general words of revocation.

on in a subsequent will [Sotheran Vs Deing 1881 20 Ch D99].

But the court may grant probate of an instrument (or part of an instrument) of a date prior to the will which contains a general revocatory clause, if it is satisfied that it was not the intention of the testator to revoke a particular legacy or permission contained in the earlier instrument [Smith vs Thompson 1931 14 TLR 603].

The revocation of a unprivileged will is an act only a little less solemn than the making of the will itself and has to comply with the statutory requirement contained in Section 70 of ISA 1925.

12.17 Conclusion

Having clearly outlined the proper execution of unprivileged wills, our next step is to review specific crucial legal provisions essential in probate proceedings. The next chapter presents the important sections of law relevant to probate cases, enhancing our comprehensive legal understanding.

Chapter 13: Important Sections in Probate Proceedings

In this chapter, we discuss important aspects of the probate of a will, such as proof of a valid will during probate proceedings and how it can be challenged. We also discuss some important court judgments related to the same.

13.1 Section 276 of ISA 1925 Petition for Probate or for letters of administration

The petition shall have the will annexed and shall be made distinctly written in English or in the language in ordinary use stating :

- The time of the testator's death

- That the writing annexed is his last will and testament

- That it was duly executed

- When the application to the district judge that the deceased at the time of his death had a fixed place of abode or had some property situated within the jurisdiction of the judge

13.2 Section 281 of ISA 1925 Verification of the petition for probate by one witness to the will

- The fund primarily liable for the payment duty is thus the residuary estate [Dayabhai v Damodardas (1922) ILR 21 Bom 75].

- It is not necessary for the applicant to pay the entire court fee (except court fee of Rs 25) while filing such a petition. Complete court fee has to be paid at the time of grant of letters of administration or probate [AIR 2010 Uttarakhand 22].

- Vagueness of the will: if the contents of the will are found to be vague despite the genuineness thereof, the grant of probate in favor of the applicant may be declined [AIR 2006 SC 1999]. Otherwise, it is not for the probate court to exercise its jurisdiction to make an interpretation of the will [2009 (1) KLJ 865]. The jurisdiction does not extend beyond the truth of execution as regards the mental capacity of the executant and the validity of attestation.

- Limitation for application of probate: The Supreme Court has held in Kanwarjeet Singh v Kirandeep [(2008) 8 SC 4] that Art 137 of the Limitation Act 1963 applies.

13.3 Important case laws

If the deceased leaves a will which names executors, the executors must apply to the probate division of the High Court for the grant of probate. This gives them official authority to act on behalf of the estate. If there is no will, the administrators of the estate will be granted "letters of administration" by the same probate division. Both grant of probate and grant of the letters of administration are referred to by a generic term: grant of representation.

Once the procedure is over, the will is a public document open to inspection by the public.

K Jaganmohan Vs D Rukhmani – AIR 2007 (NOC) 592 (MAD)

"In absence of suspicious circumstances surrounding execution, it is sufficient for propounder to discharge onus by adding proof of testamentary capacity and proof of signature."

13.4 Difference between executor and administrator

- An administrator can only be appointed by a competent court. An executor can only be appointed by the person making will or codicil.

- An executor derives his title from the will and all the property of the testator vests in him from the date of the testator's death. An administrator derives his title from the letters of administration and the property of the deceased does not vest in him until the grant [AIR 1960 AP 273, 281]

- The executor of a will capable of obtaining probate is a legal representative capable of instituting a suit from the date of the testator's death within the meaning of Art 17 of the Limitations Act / Lunatic Act, 1908, time begins to run from the date of the testator's death and not from the date of the grant of probate. But in the case of an administrator, the period does not run until the grant is made.

- An executor can give a valid discharge and do all acts for the administration of the estate before grant to probate. An administrator may not do so.

- An administrator is required to execute a bond called Administration Bond before the grant is made to him.

- A period of seven clear days is required to pass after the death of a person leaving the will or codicil before probate can be granted.

- The capacity of executors is joint and several and probate may be granted to one or more executors but the capacity of administrators is joint.

The office of an executor or administrator is not assignable, nor does it survive after the death of the sole executor or administrator.

13.5 Probate granted only to appointed executor [Section 222 of Indian Succession Act 1925]

- Probate is granted only to appointed executor (by will)

- The appointment may be expressed or by necessary implication

13.6 Summary Table of Key Sections of the Indian Succession Act

Section	Topic	Summary
63	Execution of unprivileged wills	Requires signature and two attesting witnesses
276	Petition for probate	Must include full details of the will and property
283	Powers of the court	Court can demand documents, summon witnesses

13.7 Cross-Referencing with Other Relevant Acts

- **Registration Act, 1908:** Deals with optional registration of wills.

- **Indian Evidence Act, 1872:** Governs admissibility of witness testimony and documents.

- **Income Tax Act, 1961:** Relevant for post-death taxation of assets.

13.8 Persons to whom probate / administration cannot be granted

A probate cannot be granted to a person who is a minor / of is of unsound mind [S 223/ S 236 of ISA 1925].

13.9 Miscellaneous judgements

- Effect of probate [S 227 of ISA 1925]: When granted, establishes the will from the death of the testator and renders valid all intermediate acts of the executor as such

- Bathgate and Co Ltd. Vs Reverend Hanok Ghosh [AIR 2008 Cal 165]

- "Tenant and/or licensee or occupant of property owned by deceased testatrix has no right to oppose or intervene in probate proceedings."

- Bhamvandal Vs Raj Kumar –[AIR 2003 Gan 90], [Section 239 of ISA 1925]

- "Filing of application for probate under section 237, 238, 239 of the ISA 1925 act: A probate may be granted and also an application for probate may be filed even without filing original will"

13.10 Legal Representative – Meaning thereof

Not defined in the act. CPC defines a legal representative as a person who in law represents the estate of the deceased person, and includes any person who intermeddles with the estate of the deceased.

13.11 When a will can be challenged

If certain people are dissatisfied with the outcome – either through having been left out of the will or because the intestacy rules have excluded them – they are able to challenge these arrangements.

Note: Challengers are not limited to dependents.

- Revocation: It may be claimed that the will was no longer valid because the testator had changed his mind, i.e. the will had been revoked (by a later will or codicil, or by destruction)

- Mental incapacity: It may be claimed that the deceased did not know or understand what he or she was doing, or its effect.

- Undue influence or fraud: It may be claimed that the deceased was subject to undue influence or fraud when making the will.

- Failure to provide for dependents: It may be claimed that the deceased failed to make reasonable provision for a dependent.

- Reasons for failure of testator's intentions: even if a will has left one a legacy, various factors may operate to prevent one from receiving the benefit.

- Insolvency: If the estate was insolvent, all the assets are used up in paying creditors.

13.12 Making sure a will is effective

One's will cannot be made effective on one's death unless it complies with the formalities prescribed by law.

1. Formalities: The testator or testatrix (the maker of a will) must be aged over 18. The will must be in writing. It need not be in English to be valid, if the testator is more familiar with another language.

The will should be clear and legible, though it does not have to be typed. It should not be written in pencil.

2. Signatures: The will should be signed by the testator at the end of the document. This is most important. A signature at the top of the will could be challenged.

The will must be signed by at least two witnesses. They and the testator must be in the same room at the same time, throughout the signing session. This fact should be stated in the will, and the date should be inserted.

The witnesses do not have to read the document. They do not even have to know that the document is a will, as long as they know that they are there to witness the signature of the testator.

3. Who can be witnesses: The witnesses must not be persons who are benefitting under the will. They also cannot be married to persons benefitting under the will. No witnesses should be a beneficiary under the will. If the testator is very elderly or infirm, one of the persons acting

as witness should be a doctor, who should examine him first to make sure he understands what he is doing and its implications. The doctor should be asked to keep a record of the examination. If the testator is too weak to sign, then even a mark will do provided it is made in the presence of the doctor who is acting as witness.

4. Where to keep the will: The testator should deposit the signed will in a safe place, perhaps with his solicitor or his bank. It is also possible to deposit the will in any Registry of the family division of the High Court. It is advisable that the testator tells his executor and family where he has put the will (they will not be able to see it until after the testator's death), so that delay in tracing is avoided. Alternatively, it may be kept in a safe place with personal papers at home. In no event should it be accessible to a disappointed heir.

5. Reviewing the contents of a will regularly: The provisions of a testator's will should be reviewed every five years or as his circumstances change, or there are changes in the value of his possessions. He must certainly consider making a new will when major family events occur, such as marriage, divorce, birth of a child or death of someone close to the testator.

6. Minor amendments and codicils: For minor amendments to one's will, one can consider making a codicil, which are used for the purpose of making changes to a will where there is no necessity to rewrite the whole will. Two witnesses must witness the signature to the codicil which must be signed and dated in the same way as the will.

13.13 Proof of Will

The law settled with regard to proof of a will is that the mode to prove a will does not ordinarily differ from that of proving any other document except as to the special requirement of attestation prescribed in the case of a will by Section 63 of the Indian Succession Act 1925.

For proof of will, the duty of the court shall be to examine the following legal requirements, consisting of five steps.

Under the Act, for the will to be valid:

- Should be reduced into writing

- Signed by the testator

- Shall be attested by two or more witnesses, and

- At least one attesting witness shall be examined

If these legal requirements are not found, in the eye of the law there is no will at all.

For proof of the will, the duty of the court shall be to examine the following legal requirements. It shall consider five steps –

- The first step is that if the documents produced before the court prima facie do not satisfy the legal requirements, the court need not make any further enquiry in so far as its due execution is concerned, and can negative a claim based on the said document.

- The second step is that when the legal heirs are disinherited, the court has to scrutinize the evidence with greater degree of care than usual.

- The third step would be to find out whether the testator was in a sound state of mind at the time of executing the will.

- The fourth step would be to find out whether there exists any suspicious circumstances surrounding the execution of the will.

- The fifth step is to consider whether the will that is executing is in accordance with Section 63 of the ISA 1925 Act read with Section 68 of the Evidence Act [AIR 2008 NOC 2433].

13.14 Wills: Whether to be stamped

Wills and codicils are not required to be stamped. They are exempt from stamp duty. However if a will is written on an old stamp paper, the Delhi high court observed that the propounder must explain why the will was written on a stamp paper not meant for the purpose [2011 (178) DLT 358].

13.15 Purpose of signing the will

Under Section 2(h) and Section 63(a) and (b) of ISA 1925, the purpose of signing a will is to authenticate the writing in the will containing the manner of disposition of the property on the testator's death. In other words, the writing containing the manner of disposition of property has to precede the signature of the testator. The name being written in the clause describing the identity of the writer cannot constitute the signature as required in a will [AIR 1986 All 220]. In a holograph will, the writing of the name to disclose the identity is not the signature.

13.16 Validity of disposition

Section 2(h) of the Indian Succession Act qualifies the declaration made by the testator in the will as legal, not the right, title and interest in the property bequeathed thereby. It is a well known legal proposition that the probate court cannot go into the question of title and it is the function of the probate court to see in the probate proceeding whether the will has been duly executed, whether the testator at the relevant time was in sound and disposing state of mind and whether the testator had understood the nature and effect of such disposition and put his signature and/or mark to the document at his free will and volition [AIR 2006 Cal 281-DB].

13.17 Conclusion

With a thorough understanding of these vital probate sections, we now approach the culmination of our journey through wills and probate. In the next chapter, we will discuss a few common mistakes to be avoided when writing a will.

Chapter 14: Common Mistakes in Will Writing and How to Avoid Them

Drafting a will is an essential step in ensuring your wishes are honoured after your passing. Unfortunately, mistakes in will-writing can lead to unnecessary disputes, legal challenges, and emotional distress among family members. This chapter outlines common pitfalls in writing wills and practical steps to avoid them, ensuring a clear, valid, and enforceable document.

14.1 Mistake: Not Clearly Identifying Beneficiaries

Problem: Ambiguity in naming beneficiaries can lead to disputes or unintended distributions.

Solution: Clearly identify beneficiaries using full names, relationships, addresses, and dates of birth. Clarify any nicknames or commonly used names explicitly.

14.2 Mistake: Failure to Name Alternate Beneficiaries

Problem: If a primary beneficiary predeceases the testator, assets may become subject to intestacy laws.

Solution: Always name alternate or contingent beneficiaries to account for unforeseen circumstances.

14.3 Mistake: Incorrect or Ambiguous Property Descriptions

Problem: Vague property descriptions can cause confusion, legal disputes, or court intervention.

Solution: Accurately describe assets, including property addresses, account numbers, and clear identifiers for jewellery, heirlooms, or artworks. Attach annexures if necessary.

14.4 Mistake: Selecting Unsuitable Executors

Problem: Choosing an inappropriate executor (due to age, location, competence, or relationship dynamics) can lead to inefficiency and conflict.

Solution: Select responsible, capable, and trustworthy executors. Discuss the role beforehand and consider appointing co-executors or professional executors (such as banks or solicitors).

14.5 Mistake: Improper Witness Attestation

Problem: Improper attestation or signatures by beneficiaries or their spouses as witnesses can invalidate the will.

Solution: Ensure that witnesses are independent adults who are not beneficiaries or related closely to beneficiaries. Clearly instruct witnesses on proper attestation procedures.

14.6 Mistake: Not Updating the Will Regularly

Problem: Failure to update your will after significant life changes (marriage, divorce, birth of children, asset acquisition) can lead to outdated provisions and unintended distributions.

Solution: Regularly review and update your will, especially after major life events. Clearly revoke previous wills and state the current version as the last valid will.

14.7 Mistake: Neglecting Digital Assets

Problem: Overlooking digital assets such as social media, emails, cryptocurrencies, or online banking information can complicate estate administration.

Solution: Specifically include digital assets in your will. Provide clear instructions on managing passwords, account access, and digital legacy.

14.8 Mistake: Omitting Debts and Liabilities

Problem: Neglecting debts or liabilities can lead to confusion and legal complications for executors.

Solution: Clearly document all known debts and liabilities, specifying how they should be addressed or settled upon your passing.

14.9 Mistake: Drafting a DIY Will without Adequate Knowledge

Problem: Amateur drafting without proper legal knowledge can inadvertently create invalid or contestable provisions.

Solution: Seek legal advice or professional drafting services, especially if your estate is complex or significant in size.

14.10 Practical Checklist to Avoid Common Will-Writing Mistakes

To summarize, here is a practical checklist to ensure the validity and clarity of your will:

- Clearly identify all beneficiaries and alternates.
- Precisely describe all assets and properties.
- Select capable executors.
- Use appropriate, unbiased witnesses.
- Regularly update your will.

- Include digital assets explicitly.

- List debts and liabilities.

- Consult a legal professional for drafting and reviewing.

14.11 Conclusion

Avoiding these common mistakes ensures that your wishes are clearly communicated, legally sound, and easily enforceable. In the next chapter, we will explore the role and responsibilities of executors, guiding you further in safeguarding your estate.

Chapter 15: Role, Duties, and Liabilities of an Executor

Choosing an executor is one of the most significant decisions you will make when writing your will. The executor is tasked with managing your estate, carrying out your wishes, and ensuring legal compliance after your death. This chapter clarifies the executor's roles, outlines key responsibilities, and illustrates common scenarios to help you understand and fulfil this vital role.

15.1 Who is an Executor?

An executor is the individual or entity appointed in your will responsible for executing its instructions, settling your estate, and ensuring that your assets are distributed according to your wishes.

15.2 Key Legal Responsibilities of an Executor

The executor's responsibilities include:

- Locating, validating, and securing the latest will.
- Filing for probate with the appropriate court.
- Identifying, securing, and managing assets.
- Paying estate debts, liabilities, and taxes.
- Notifying beneficiaries and distributing assets according to the will.
- Maintaining accurate records and preparing estate accounts.

15.3 Practical Duties of an Executor

In addition to legal responsibilities, executors perform numerous practical tasks:

- Obtaining certified copies of death certificates.

- Closing bank accounts and transferring funds.

- Managing or disposing of properties and assets.

- Settling utility bills, subscriptions, and debts.

- Coordinating with lawyers, accountants, and financial institutions.

15.4 Common Challenges and How to Address Them

Scenario 1: Disputes among beneficiaries

- Issue: Beneficiaries disagree over asset distribution.

- Resolution: Transparent communication, regular updates, and impartial mediation can help prevent disputes. When disagreements persist, an executor may involve legal counsel or consider mediation services.

Scenario 2: Managing debts exceeding the estate value

- Issue: Estate debts are higher than asset value, causing concerns among beneficiaries.

- Resolution: The executor must prioritize debts as per legal guidelines. Inform creditors and beneficiaries transparently about insolvency and seek legal advice on managing insolvency proceedings.

Scenario 3: Locating missing assets or documents

- Issue: Difficulty in identifying or locating the deceased's assets.

- Resolution: Executors should methodically review financial statements, contact institutions directly, and seek professional assistance from lawyers or financial advisors.

15.5 Liabilities of an Executor

Executors may incur personal liability if they:

- Fail to act diligently or responsibly.

- Mishandle estate assets or neglect debts and taxes.

- Distribute assets prematurely without settling liabilities.

To mitigate these risks, executors should:

- Maintain meticulous records.

- Seek professional advice where necessary.

- Ensure transparency with beneficiaries and the probate court.

15.6 Real-life Scenario Illustrations

Scenario: Executor unaware of outstanding debts

- Problem: An executor distributed estate assets to beneficiaries without clearing the deceased's outstanding loan, resulting in legal claims from creditors.

- Solution: Executors must thoroughly investigate all possible debts and wait until debts and liabilities are settled or accounted for before asset distribution. Legal counsel can guide the proper process.

Scenario: Dispute due to delayed asset distribution

- Problem: Beneficiaries accuse the executor of intentional delays.

- Solution: The executor should maintain clear records documenting reasons for delays and regularly communicate updates to beneficiaries. Transparency helps reduce misunderstandings and potential disputes.

15.7 Executor's Checklist for Effective Estate Management

- Validate and secure the latest version of the will.

- Initiate probate proceedings promptly.

- Conduct comprehensive asset inventory and valuation.

- Settle outstanding debts, liabilities, and taxes.

- Maintain clear, documented records and accounts.

- Ensure regular, transparent communication with beneficiaries.

- Seek professional advice whenever uncertainty arises.

15.8 Conclusion

The role of executor, while demanding, is essential for honouring a testator's wishes and ensuring the smooth administration of an estate. Understanding and proactively managing these responsibilities helps executors fulfil their duties efficiently, legally, and ethically. In our next chapter, we will explore managing digital assets, an increasingly critical aspect of modern estate planning.

Chapter 16: Digital Assets and Wills: Handling Your Digital Legacy

In today's digital age, a significant portion of our lives exists online—emails, social media accounts, online banking, cryptocurrencies, digital wallets, and various subscriptions. These digital assets require careful handling within the context of estate planning. This chapter explores the management and secure transfer of digital assets through your will, ensuring that your digital legacy is preserved and responsibly administered.

16.1 What are Digital Assets?

Digital assets include any online accounts, electronically stored information, or assets held digitally, such as:

- Email accounts
- Social media profiles (Facebook, Instagram, LinkedIn, Twitter)
- Online banking and brokerage accounts
- Digital wallets and cryptocurrencies (Bitcoin, Ethereum, etc.)
- Cloud storage (Google Drive, Dropbox, iCloud)
- E-commerce accounts (Amazon, Flipkart)
- Digital content subscriptions (Netflix, Spotify)

16.2 Importance of Including Digital Assets in Your Will

Neglecting digital assets can lead to difficulties in accessing crucial information, potential financial losses, or identity theft. Including clear provisions for these assets in your will:

- Provides explicit directions to your executor.

- Prevents potential loss of assets.

- Ensures proper closure or continuation of online accounts.

- Protects your digital identity and privacy posthumously.

16.3 Indian Legal Framework and Digital Assets

Under Indian law, digital assets, particularly financial ones like cryptocurrencies, fall under the ambit of movable property. Thus, they are transferable through a will, provided:

- Clear identification and access instructions are given.

- The executor is empowered explicitly to manage and transfer these digital assets.

- Legal compliance, including taxation (where applicable), is addressed.

16.4 How to Incorporate Digital Assets in Your Will

Your will should clearly specify:

- A comprehensive list of digital assets and their access points (not passwords).

- Instructions for managing each type of digital asset.

- The appointed digital executor or person specifically tasked with handling digital assets.

Note: For security, passwords should never be included directly in a will. Instead, use a secure, encrypted password manager, providing access instructions separately to your executor.

16.5 Practical Recommendations for Secure Digital Asset Transfer

Some practical recommendations include the following:

- Use a Digital Inventory: Maintain a regularly updated, detailed digital asset inventory with descriptions and access methods.

- Designate a Digital Executor: Appoint someone familiar with technology and online security to handle digital assets efficiently.

- Employ a Secure Password Manager: Securely store passwords and digital keys in an encrypted password management tool. Provide your executor with the means to access this securely.

- Regularly Update Information: Update your digital assets list and access methods regularly, notifying your executor about significant changes.

- Clarify Your Wishes Clearly: Indicate whether digital accounts should be closed, memorialized (for social media), or transferred to beneficiaries.

16.6 Real-Life Scenario Illustration

Scenario: Accessing Cryptocurrency Assets

- Problem: An individual passed away without providing access to his cryptocurrency wallet, resulting in significant asset loss for his family.

- Solution: Clear documentation of wallet details and secure private key storage with access instructions provided separately to the executor would have prevented this loss.

Scenario: Social Media Management Post-Death

- Problem: A social media profile of a deceased individual was left unmanaged, causing emotional distress to family members.

- Solution: Explicit instructions in the will to either memorialize, delete, or transfer the management of social media accounts can offer clarity and emotional relief.

16.7 Executor Checklist for Digital Assets

- Verify the inclusion of digital assets explicitly in the will.

- Obtain the digital assets inventory and password manager access.

- Follow detailed instructions for asset management provided in the will.

- Handle digital accounts according to specified wishes (closing, memorializing, transferring).

- Consult IT experts or legal professionals if encountering difficulties.

16.8 Conclusion

Effectively managing your digital legacy is an essential component of comprehensive estate planning. By incorporating explicit instructions for digital assets in your will and adopting recommended security practices, you ensure seamless asset transfer, safeguard your digital identity, and minimize complications for your beneficiaries. The next chapter expands on other estate planning tools beyond wills, specifically exploring trusts.

Chapter 17: E-Wills and Digital Execution

The digital age has transformed the way we live, communicate, and manage our financial affairs. In recent years, it has also begun to reshape how we plan for succession and execute wills. With increased use of technology in personal and professional domains, the question arises: can wills be made, executed, and stored electronically in India? What are the legal and practical implications of so-called "E-Wills"?

This chapter explores the emerging world of electronic wills (e-wills), their current legal status in India, international developments, and best practices for those considering the digital route.

17.1 What is an E-Will?

An electronic will (e-will) is a will that is created, signed, and stored in digital form, rather than on paper. It may involve:

- Drafting the will using online platforms or legal tech services.

- Execution (signing and attestation) using digital signatures, electronic records, or video conferencing.

- Storing the will in digital repositories or on the cloud.

The concept promises convenience, accessibility, and security—but it also raises concerns about validity, authenticity, and privacy.

17.2 Legal Status of E-Wills in India

a) Indian Succession Act Requirements

As discussed earlier in this book, under the Indian Succession Act, 1925, a valid will must be:

- In writing (except for certain oral wills in rare cases).

- Signed by the testator (or by someone else in the testator's presence and direction).

- Attested by at least two witnesses, who see the testator sign or receive a personal acknowledgment.

The law does not specifically provide for digital or electronic wills. The requirements have always been interpreted to mean a physical, handwritten, or printed document with wet-ink signatures and physical witness attestation.

b) Electronic Signatures and the IT Act

The Information Technology Act, 2000 recognizes electronic signatures and electronic records for most documents, but expressly excludes wills and testamentary dispositions from its scope (see Section 1(4) and the First Schedule).

Therefore:

- E-wills are not explicitly valid in India as of now.

- Wills signed using a digital signature, or executed solely in electronic form, may not be accepted by Indian probate courts.

17.3 E-Wills in Practice: What is Happening in India?

Despite the lack of formal recognition, a growing number of private service providers offer "online will-making" or "digital will storage" services. Typically, these services work as follows:

- The testator uses an online platform to draft a will.

- The document is then printed and executed in the traditional manner: signed in ink, attested by two witnesses.

- Some services offer secure digital storage or allow for video-recording of the will-signing for evidence.

Note:

- The end product, to be legally enforceable, is still a paper will, properly signed and witnessed.

- Digital records, video recordings, or cloud storage may help as secondary evidence, but do not replace the statutory requirements.

17.4 International Trends and Comparisons

Some countries, notably the USA, Australia, and the UK, have begun to experiment with legalizing e-wills, particularly in response to the COVID-19 pandemic.

- United States: Some states (e.g., Nevada, Florida, Arizona) have enacted laws recognizing electronic wills signed and attested online, subject to strict procedures and identity checks.

- United Kingdom: Emergency pandemic legislation temporarily allowed remote witnessing of wills via video link.

- Australia: Certain states permit electronic execution of wills under specific conditions.

These developments signal the possibility that Indian law may evolve in the future, but as of now, Indian courts do not recognize e-wills.

17.5 Video Wills and Digital Evidence

Some individuals choose to record a video of themselves reading out their will or explaining its terms. While a video will is not a substitute for a written, attested document, it can:

- Serve as supporting evidence of the testator's mental capacity and voluntariness.

- Help dispel doubts about undue influence or coercion.

- Reduce the chances of disputes among heirs.

However, unless accompanied by a properly executed written will, a video recording alone does not meet the requirements for a valid will under Indian law.

17.6 Blockchain and Future Technologies

Emerging technologies like blockchain promise even greater security and verifiability for digital wills. Some jurisdictions are experimenting with registering wills on blockchain networks to create tamper-proof records. For now, these innovations remain in the realm of pilot projects and are not yet legally recognized in India.

17.7 Best Practices for Tech-Savvy Testators in India

Some best practices for testators include:

- Use Online Drafting Tools with Caution: They can simplify the process, but always print the final version for manual signing and attestation.

- Do Not Rely on Digital Signatures Alone: Courts may reject a will not physically signed and witnessed as required by law.

- Store Paper Originals Safely: Keep the signed original in a secure, accessible place; inform your executor and trusted family members.

- Supplement with Digital Evidence: Video-record the execution, store copies in the cloud, or notify beneficiaries—these can help support the will's validity if contested.

- Stay Informed: Watch for legal developments as law and technology evolve in India.

17.8 Recommendations for Lawmakers and the Future

There is a growing need for Indian law to keep pace with technology.

Law Commissions and expert bodies have recommended exploring the recognition of e-wills, with safeguards to prevent fraud and coercion.

Any future reform should strike a balance between convenience and the need for certainty, security, and protection of vulnerable persons.

17.9 Conclusion

While e-wills and digital execution offer exciting possibilities for the future, as of today, a will in India must comply with traditional requirements: a written document, signed in ink, and attested by two witnesses. Technology can assist in drafting, storing, and evidencing wills, but cannot yet replace the paper original. Testators and their advisors should use digital tools with care and always ensure their wills meet the legal requirements to avoid future disputes.

Chapter 18: Trusts and Estate Planning Beyond Wills

While a will serves as a fundamental tool for estate planning, trusts can complement wills by providing additional benefits such as asset protection, tax efficiency, and controlled asset distribution. This chapter explores trusts, their benefits in family and charitable contexts, and practical steps for establishing a trust in India.

18.1 Understanding Trusts in Estate Planning

A trust is a legal arrangement where one person (the settlor) transfers ownership of assets to another person or entity (the trustee) to manage these assets for the benefit of a third party (beneficiary). Trusts can operate both during your lifetime and after your death, making them valuable for comprehensive estate planning.

18.2 Types of Trusts Commonly Used in India

- **Private Trust:** Created for the benefit of specific individuals, typically family members.

- **Public (Charitable) Trust:** Created for public benefit, such as education, relief of poverty, healthcare, or religious purposes.

- **Testamentary Trust:** Formed through a will, becoming effective after the settlor's death.

- **Living Trust (Inter Vivos Trust):** Established during the lifetime of the settlor.

18.3 Benefits of Family and Charitable Trusts

Family Trusts:

- Protect family wealth from creditors and litigation.

- Ensure controlled distribution of assets to beneficiaries.

- Provide for minors or beneficiaries unable to manage finances responsibly.

- Reduce estate and inheritance taxes.

Charitable Trusts:

- Facilitate structured and transparent charitable contributions.

- Provide tax exemptions and deductions under Indian law.

- Ensure sustainable funding and governance of charitable activities.

- Create a lasting philanthropic legacy.

18.4 Key Differences Between Wills and Trusts

The following table gives the key differences between wills and trusts.

Aspect	Will	Trust
Probate	Required	Avoided
Privacy	Public record after probate	Private
Asset Management	Post-death only	Both during life and after death
Modification	Easily modified by testator	Depends on type and terms of trust
Asset Protection	Limited	Enhanced asset protection

18.5 Practical Steps for Establishing a Trust in India

Some practical steps before establishing a trust include:

1. **Determine Purpose:** Clearly define the trust's objective (family welfare, education, charity, etc.).

2. **Choose Trustees:** Select trustworthy and capable individuals or professional entities.

3. **Draft the Trust Deed:** Clearly articulate terms, objectives, trustee powers, beneficiary details, and asset management guidelines.

4. **Fund the Trust:** Transfer assets legally and explicitly to the trust.

5. **Registration:** Register the trust deed with the appropriate sub-registrar as per Indian Trusts Act, 1882 (for private trusts) or relevant state laws (for charitable trusts).

6. **Manage Compliance:** Ensure ongoing legal, regulatory, and tax compliance.

18.6 Legal Requirements for Establishing Trusts in India

Some legal requirements to keep in mind while establishing a trust in India include the following:

- **Trust Deed:** Must be clearly written, stating objectives, trustee duties, beneficiary identification, and asset management.

- **Settlor's Capacity:** Must be legally competent to transfer property.

- **Trustee Acceptance:** Trustees must explicitly accept their duties.

- **Property Transfer:** Clearly transfer the legal title of assets to the trust.

- **Registration Compliance:** Mandatory registration for charitable trusts and recommended for private trusts for legal validity and enforceability.

18.7 Real-Life Scenario Illustrations

Scenario: Family Trust for Minor Children

- Situation: Parents concerned about future financial management for minor children.

- Solution: Establish a family trust that specifies regular payments to guardians, education expenses, and structured inheritance once minors reach maturity.

Scenario: Charitable Trust for Education

- Situation: An individual wishes to dedicate their wealth towards education after their death.

- Solution: Establish a charitable trust during their lifetime or through their will, clearly outlining the educational purpose, governance structure, and funding mechanism.

18.8 Checklist for Establishing a Trust

- Define clear objectives.

- Select reliable trustees.

- Draft and execute a comprehensive trust deed.

- Register the trust appropriately.

- Ensure continuous compliance with legal and tax regulations.

- Regularly review and update trust provisions as required.

18.9 Conclusion

Trusts serve as powerful instruments that complement wills in estate planning, offering enhanced asset protection, controlled distribution, tax benefits, and opportunities for lasting philanthropic impact. Properly establishing and maintaining a trust can significantly benefit your beneficiaries and fulfil your long-term estate planning objectives. In the following chapter, we explore the financial and taxation aspects of estate planning, emphasizing estate duty, tax implications, and financial management strategies.

Chapter 19: Estate Tax and Financial Implications

While wills and trusts determine how your estate is distributed, understanding the tax implications is equally essential. Estate planning in India must take into account income tax, capital gains, and stamp duty consequences, even though India currently does not levy a separate estate duty or inheritance tax. This chapter discusses the key financial considerations and practical strategies to minimize tax impact.

19.1 Understanding Taxation in Estate Planning

In India, estate duty was abolished in 1985. However, various other taxes and financial obligations may still apply:

- Income Tax: Income generated by the estate post-death is taxed.

- Capital Gains Tax: Triggered upon sale or transfer of property inherited.

- Stamp Duty: Applies on the transfer or registration of property.

- Wealth Tax: Abolished in 2015 but replaced by a surcharge on high-income earners.

19.2 Tax Treatment of Inherited Assets

- Inheritance itself is not taxed.

- However, sale of inherited property attracts capital gains tax.

- Assets are considered as acquired at the cost and date of acquisition by the original owner for tax purposes (indexed cost).

19.3 Strategies for Tax-Efficient Estate Planning

- Use of Trusts: Can help distribute income over time, potentially reducing the tax burden on beneficiaries.

- Gifts During Lifetime: Gifting assets before death (within exemptions) may help reduce potential tax liabilities.

- Joint Ownership: Helps in smooth succession, particularly for bank accounts and real estate.

- Nominations: Ensure financial assets like insurance, mutual funds, and bank accounts are transferred efficiently.

- Capital Gains Planning: Time asset sales strategically and use exemptions under Sections 54, 54F, etc.

19.4 Financial Impacts: With and Without Proper Estate Planning

Example 1: Without Planning

- A family discovers that a deceased parent's property is not registered in their name.

- No will or nomination exists.

- The property transfer incurs high stamp duty and litigation costs.

- Delays cause rental income loss and emotional stress.

Example 2: With Planning

- A will clearly transfers property to the spouse.

- Nomination in bank accounts enables smooth fund access.

- Mutual fund units passed efficiently with proper nominations.

- Capital gains are planned and spread over two financial years, saving significant tax.

19.5 Practical Checklist for Financially Smart Estate Planning

- Draft and update your will regularly.

- Declare and nominate all financial instruments.

- Consider creating a private trust for large or complex assets.

- Maintain updated documentation for real estate, investments, and insurances.

- Consult tax and legal professionals to align your estate plan with financial efficiency.

19.6 Conclusion

Estate planning is not just about who gets what—it's about how efficiently and responsibly your wealth is passed on. By proactively addressing tax implications and using available legal tools, you can preserve wealth and reduce burdens for your loved ones.

Chapter 20: Alternative Dispute Resolution (ADR) for Probate Matters

Estate disputes can be emotionally draining, time-consuming, and expensive. Alternative Dispute Resolution (ADR) methods offer a constructive way to resolve probate and inheritance conflicts outside the traditional courtroom setting. This chapter explores the role of mediation, conciliation, and arbitration in probate matters and provides guidance on effectively using these tools to maintain family harmony and save resources.

20.1 What is ADR?

ADR refers to techniques that resolve disputes without formal litigation. The most common forms of ADR in India are:

- Mediation: A neutral third party facilitates a mutually acceptable solution.

- Conciliation: Similar to mediation but often involves more active suggestions by the conciliator.

- Arbitration: A neutral arbitrator hears both sides and makes a binding decision.

20.2 Advantages of ADR in Probate Matters

The advantages of alternative dispute mechanisms include:

- Cost-Effective: Avoids heavy legal fees and court costs.

- Time-Saving: Faster than formal litigation which can drag on for years.

- Preserves Relationships: Encourages cooperative rather than adversarial outcomes.

- Confidential: Proceedings remain private, unlike public court records.

- Flexible: Informal settings allow more creative and tailored solutions.

20.3 Types of Probate Disputes Suitable for ADR

Suitable types of disputes include:

- Disputes between legal heirs or beneficiaries.

- Objections regarding asset distribution.

- Conflicts over interpretation of ambiguous will clauses.

- Claims by omitted or estranged family members.

- Disagreements about executor conduct or performance.

20.4 Real-Life Scenario Illustrations

Scenario 1: Family Conflict Over Inheritance Shares

- Problem: Two siblings contest the division of property mentioned in the will.

- ADR Solution: A mediator helps facilitate honest communication, leading to a compromise that satisfies both parties, avoiding court litigation.

Scenario 2: Contesting Executor Decisions

- Problem: A beneficiary accuses the executor of mismanaging estate funds.

- ADR Solution: Conciliation helps clarify misunderstandings and sets mutual expectations, saving the executor from a court summons.

20.5 Choosing the Right ADR Mechanism

- Mediation: Best for emotionally charged disputes and preserving relationships.

- Conciliation: Suitable when expert guidance is needed but with a non-binding outcome.

- Arbitration: Appropriate when parties seek a binding resolution without going to court.

20.6 Practical Tips for Navigating ADR in Probate Matters

- Select an experienced ADR professional familiar with probate and inheritance law.

- Set clear goals: Are you seeking reconciliation, clarification, or a binding decision?

- Ensure all relevant parties and documents are present during ADR sessions.

- Prepare emotionally—listen actively and negotiate respectfully.

- Document all agreements reached and, where necessary, seek court validation.

20.7 Legal Recognition of ADR in India

- Section 89 of the Civil Procedure Code, 1908 encourages courts to refer disputes to ADR.

- The Arbitration and Conciliation Act, 1996 provides a framework for enforceable ADR agreements.

- Mediation is increasingly promoted in Indian family courts and Lok Adalats.

20.8 Conclusion

ADR offers a valuable alternative to contentious and costly litigation in probate matters. By choosing mediation, conciliation, or arbitration, families can resolve disputes amicably, preserve relationships, and honour the intent of the deceased without prolonged court battles.

Chapter 21: Conclusion

In this book, we have explored the essential principles and practical processes surrounding wills and probate under Indian law. From the preliminary considerations in drafting a will to the intricacies of probate proceedings, each chapter was designed to guide you step-by-step through the legal and procedural dimensions of estate planning.

We began by discussing the significance of writing a clear and valid will, the legal formalities to be observed, and the importance of choosing suitable executors and witnesses. We then examined what happens before and after the testator's death, including the responsibilities of executors and the necessary documentation to initiate probate.

Subsequent chapters focused on the structure and interpretation of a will, how courts assess the testator's intent, and common grounds on which wills are challenged—such as fraud, coercion, or lack of mental capacity. We also looked at procedural aspects like filing a probate petition, the execution of unprivileged wills, and key sections of the Indian Succession Act.

Importantly, we expanded the discussion beyond traditional wills, offering insights on digital assets, the role of trusts in estate planning, tax considerations, and alternative dispute resolution mechanisms. Through real-life scenarios, practical checklists, and legal guidance, we have aimed to make this book both informative and accessible.

This book is intended to serve as a foundational guide for anyone involved in estate planning—whether you are writing a will, executing one, or navigating the probate process after the loss of a loved one. It is our hope that with this knowledge, you can plan more confidently, prevent future disputes, and protect the interests of your family and beneficiaries.

In a world where family dynamics, digital assets, and legal complexities continue to evolve, proactive estate planning is not just wise—it is essential. Let this book be your first step toward securing your legacy with clarity, compassion, and legal foresight.

Glossary of important terms related to wills

Administrator: A person appointed by a competent authority (court) to administer the estate of a deceased person when there is no executor.

Appellant: The party who appeals a decision of a lower court, usually that of a trial court.

Appellee: The party against whom an appeal is made (sometimes referred to as a respondent - a person who defends in an appeal).

Beneficiary: A person for whose benefit a will, trust, insurance policy or contract is made.

Bequest: In a will, a gift by the testator of a specific personal property other than money.

Codicil: An instrument made in relation to a will and explaining, altering or adding to its dispositions and shall be deemed to form part of the will.

Cause of action: A person's right to seek a remedy when his or her rights have been breached and violated.

Damages: The monetary loss suffered by a party as a result of a wrong. Compensation for such damage may be claimed, depending on the circumstances, in a court of law.

Decedent: A person deceased

Decedents: The lineal heir of a decedent in a descending line - children and grandchildren.

Deed: The document representing ownership of real property.

Defamation: Injury of a person's character or reputation, usually by publication of a false statement about that person.

Defendant: The party who defends the initial action brought against him or her by the plaintiff.

Devise: A term of conveyance in a real estate transaction in a will, a gift of real estate by the testator is a device.

Executor / executrix: The personal representative of a testator's will to dispose of an estate as the will has directed.

Forgery: A fraudulent fake instrument or document or signature of another without authorization.

Fraud: An intentional or reckless misrepresentation of a material fact that causes anyone relying on it injury or damages.

Fraudulent conveyance: The transfer of property in such a manner that the conveyance is deemed either in fact or by law to defraud creditors.

Law: Enforceable rules governing the relationship of individuals and persons, their relationship to each other and other relationship to an organized society.

Legacy: In a will, a specific gift of money — money passing under a will, inheritance through a will.

Probate: The legal procedure by which a deceased person's property is inventoried and apprised, claims against the estate are paid and remaining property is distributed to the heirs under the will or according to state law if there is no will, proof established by procedure e.g. probate of a will.

Plaintiff: The party who initiates an action at law and who seeks a specified remedy.

Procedural Law: The rules for carrying on a lawsuit (pleading, evidence, jurisdictional as opposed to substantive law).

Revocation: In contract law, the withdrawing of an offer by the offerer.

Substantive law: The basic rights and duties of parties as provided for in any field of law, as opposed to procedural law under which these rights and duties are determined in a lawsuit.

Testamentary capacity: The state of mind of a testator in knowing what property is owned and how he or she wants to dispose of it.

Testate: The situation in which a person dies leaving a valid will

Undue influence: The overcoming of a person's free will by misusing a position of confidence or relationship, thereby taking advantage of that person to affect his or her decision or actions.

Will: A document by which a person directs the disposition of his or her property (Estate) upon his or her death.

Domicile: The country or legal jurisdiction that a person treats as their permanent home. Domicile is a key determinant of which law governs succession to movable property.

Estate: The total assets, property, and liabilities left behind by a deceased person, administered by the executor or administrator before distribution to beneficiaries.

Holographic Will: A will entirely handwritten and signed by the testator. Indian courts recognise a strong presumption of genuineness in favour of holographic wills.

Intestate: The condition of dying without a valid will. Property of an intestate person is distributed according to statutory rules of intestate succession.

Letters of Administration: A court document granting authority to an administrator to manage and distribute the estate of a person who died without appointing an executor, or whose executor is unable to act.

Nomination: The designation of a person (nominee) to receive benefits from a financial account, insurance policy, or provident fund on the account holder's death. Nomination is distinct from testamentary inheritance and is governed by the relevant special statute.

Onus Probandi: *(Latin: burden of proof)* In probate proceedings, the onus probandi lies on the party propounding the will to satisfy the court that it is the valid last will of a free and capable testator.

Propounder: The person who puts forward a will for probate, typically an executor or beneficiary named in the will who seeks to establish its validity before a court.

Residuary Estate: The portion of the estate remaining after all specific bequests, debts, taxes, and administration expenses have been met. A well-drafted will names a residuary beneficiary to receive whatever is left over.

Testamentary Trust: A trust created within a will that comes into effect on the testator's death. It is commonly used to hold assets for minor beneficiaries or to provide structured income to dependants over time.

Trust: A legal arrangement in which one party (the trustee) holds and manages assets for the benefit of another (the beneficiary). Trusts in India are governed primarily by the Indian Trusts Act, 1882.

Witness: A person who observes the testator signing the will and then signs it as confirmation. Under Section 63 of the Indian Succession Act 1925, at least two witnesses are required for an unprivileged will; no witness should also be a beneficiary under the will.

About the author

Siva Prasad Bose is an author of introductory guidebooks on aspects of Indian laws. He is currently retired after many years of service in Uttar Pradesh Power Corporation Limited (UPPCL, formerly UPSEB). He received his engineering degree from Jadavpur University, Kolkata and has a law degree from Meerut University, Meerut. His interests lie in the fields of family law, civil law, law of contracts, and areas of law related to electricity grid and revenue related issues. He lives in New Delhi.

Other books by Siva Prasad Bose

Introduction to Wills and Probate

Senior Citizens Abuse in India

Introduction to negotiable instruments

Introduction to marriage laws in India

Neighbor Problems in India and what to do about them

Managing Court Cases with Mental Strength

Delays in Court Cases in India

Introduction to Patents and Patent Law in India